WE'VE GOT A JOB TO DO

CHICAGOANS AND WORLD WAR II

Perry R. Duis and Scott La France

Chicago Historical Society

The exhibition *Chicago Goes to War, 1941–45* was on view at the
Chicago Historical Society from May 23, 1992, to August 15, 1993.

Published in the United States of America in
1992 by the Chicago Historical Society.
©1992 by the Chicago Historical Society.

Director of Publications, Chicago Historical Society: Russell Lewis.
Edited by Rosemary Adams and Patricia Bereck Weikersheimer.
Designed by Bill Van Nimwegen. Composed in Futura with Bodoni
book titles. Art produced on a Macintosh IIci with Quark Xpress,
Adobe Illustrator, and Adobe Photoshop. Printed by Great Lakes
Graphics, Inc., Skokie, Illinois.

Library of Congress Cataloging-in-Publication Data:
Duis, Perry, 1943–
     We've got a job to do : Chicagoans and World War II /
by Perry Duis and Scott La France.
     p.   cm.
     Includes bibliographical references and index.
     ISBN 0-913820-17-2
     1. World War, 1939–1945—Illinois—Chicago. 2.
     Chicago (Ill.)—History. I. La France, Scott, 1960– . II. Title.
D769.85.I3D85 1992   92-14491
977.3'11042—dc20   CIP

Cover: adaptation of poster by Samuel Greenburg, 1942.
Inside cover: photograph by Stephen Deutsch, a prominent Chicago
advertising photographer. Deutsch made this striking photograph to
graphically show the wartime conversion of a local hairpin factory to
a munitions production facility.

Contents

The following individuals and institutions provided assistance, knowledge, and/or artifacts to the exhibition *Chicago Goes to War, 1941–45*

Lynn Abbie
Abbott Laboratories
Christina Adachi
Patti Adachi
Paul Adler
Laura Ahuett
Matilda Ainchum
Albert Kahn Associates
ALCOA
All Style Iron Products, Inc.
Arthur Albach in memory of August Albach
Mrs. Solomon Alpert
James Alter
Amco Corporation
American National Can Company
American Red Cross—National Capital Chapter
The American Science Center
Pat Amino
Amtrak
William Anderson
Simon Andrews
Jesse Arbor
Kenneth M. Arenberg
Mrs. Milton K. Arenberg
Mary Edith Arnold
Patrick Ashley
Mr. and Mrs. Henry L. Ashworth
AT&T
The Austin Company
Loretta S. Backman
Mrs. Arthur R. Baer
Ball Corporation
Balzekas Museum of Lithuanian Culture
Gail Barazani
Ramon F. Barba
Vincent Barba
Barber-Greene Company
Barr Company
Steve Bartkowski
BBC Sound Archives
Kenneth Becker
Bell & Howell Company
R. Ford Bentley
Brian Bergheger
Herman Berghoff
Mrs. Charles Berman in memory of Sidney Berman
Rabbi Howard A. Berman
Frank R. Berninger
Allen Berns
Michael Biddle
Mr. and Mrs. Edwin Bielski

Richard Bitterman
Mrs. Essie T. Blaylock
Jeraldene Bloom
Bloom Township High School
Charles Branham
Joseph Breitenbucher
Miss Jean Brooks
Catherine Bruck
Mrs. Henry Buchbinder
Edward C. Bunting
Mrs. Donald Burns
Shirley Burton
Brother John Bush
Helen Gertrude Burt in memory of Harry L. Burt
The C.H. Hanson Company
Susan L. Caillouet in memory of Rudolf Baldanzi
John L. Caruso
Maureen Cassaro
Cynthia Certik
Chicago & Northwestern Historical Society
Chicago Car
Chicago Jewish Archives
Chicago Jewish Historical Society
Chicago Park District Special Collections
Chicago Public Library
Chicago Shimpo
Chicago Sinai Congregation
Chicago Sun-Times Inc.
Chicago Tribune
Chrysler Corp.
Grace Chun
The Cincinnati Historical Society
Phillip M. Citrin
Karen Clausen
Patricia Collins
Dick Condon
Marilou Cosgrove
COSI, Ohio's Center of Science & Industry
Marilyn Cota
Willa G. Cramton
Jeff Crisman
Maria Cunningham
Mary Jane Curran
Steve Cushing
Joseph A. Dahlia
Gerald Danzer
Vince Dawson
Antonio Delgado
Karen Deller
Stephen G. Dinsmore
Albert Dorsch
Mrs. John P. Dubsky
Perry R. Duis
DuPage County Historical Museum
The DuSable Museum of African-American History, Inc.

EAA Aviation Foundation
Donald Edelmann
Edelmann/Stant Corporation
Elmhurst Historical Museum
Rudolph and Berenice Emmering
Dr. Ann Englander
Myra Epping
Isabel Ernst
Ernst & Young
Esquire
The Evans-Tibbs Collection
Evanston Historical Society
John J. Farmer
Audrey Faulhaber
Terry Fife/History Works Inc.
Dr. Oscar Fitzgerald
Michael FitzSimmons
Forest Park Mall
Earl L. Forman
Fort Sheridan Museum
The Franklin D. Roosevelt Library
Prudence Fuchsman
Dennis Gabel
Lynne Galli
Connie Garringer
Gerald Gidwitz
Eunice Glos
Anita Gold
Mrs. Stanley C. Golder
Gordon Goldman
Thomas and Susan Gamnes
Nancy Gramse
Mr. and Mrs. Joseph Greenwald
Chief Roy Griggs
Lee and Sandee Grossman
Robert Guritz in memory of Grace King
Timothy Hagan
John Halvorsen and Richard Halvorsen in memory of Soren and Esther Halvorsen
Cornelius Hamel
Fritz Hamer
Ray Hansen
Mack Harbin
Pam Harkins
Harry S. Truman Library
Ursula Hartge
Susan Hartmann
Irene Hartwig
Lucile Rudoy Hauser
Hebrew Union College, Skirball Museum
Doreen Hedberg
Mrs. Jane Heidank
Cindy Heisler
Hans Heitman
Helene Curtis Industries, Inc.
Donald Helgeson
Sonya M. Helmer
Lorraine Hempe

Henry Ford Museum and Greenfield Village
Idrienne L. Heymann
Lynn Hieatt
Edward Hines, Jr., VA Hospital
Marlene M. Hinsch
James Hirabayashi
Historical Museum of Addison
Historical Society of Cicero
The Historical Society of Forest Park
Nathan Hoffman
Melvin G. Holli
Fred Hollman
Honeywell, Inc.
Hoover Historical Center
Robert Hornstein in memory of Henry H. Hornstein
Sylvia Hornstein in memory of Henry H. Hornstein
Allen H. Howard
Bernard Howard
Barbara Hrdina
Ralph Huszagh
George A. Iberle
Illinois Auto Electric Company
Illinois State Archives
Leonard Impastato
JeAnne Ingersoll in memory of her sister, Gloria
Ralph Isaacsen
Loraine P. Isenberger in memory of Lois Loraine Sherman
Cecilia T. Ishibashi
Daniel Jackson
Richard Jaffe
Gayle Janowitz in memory of Morris Janowitz
Virginia Jansen
Lillian Janus
The Japanese American Citizens League
Stephen Jarzyna
Helen Jaworski
Dorothy Johnsen
Peter Johnsen
Royna Rogers Johnson
Virgil Johnson
Mr. and Mrs. Jeffrey Jones
Thomas L. Jones
Mr. and Mrs. Theodore Karamanski
Theodore J. Karamanski and Eileen McMahon
Richard Kapelinski
Bernice Narbut Kaufmann
Donald Keane
Dr. Geraldine Augustyn Kearns
Eric A. Keeley
Andrew J. Kelleher
Paul Kelly, Illinois Recycling Center
Elizabeth M. Kenny
Ester Kenny

The exhibition *Chicago Goes to War, 1941–45*
was made possible in part through the generosity of:

Robert R. McCormick Tribune Foundation

Oil-Dri Corporation of America

MIDCON Corporation

GATX Corporation

Hal Riney & Partners, Inc.

Pepsi-Cola Company

Illinois Humanities Council

The National Endowment for the Humanities,
  a federal agency

Preface

Russell Lewis

When Americans went to war more than fifty years ago, no one could anticipate the full consequences on his or her life and on generations to follow. Uncertainty abounded. Nobody knew how long the war would last, when and if loved ones would return home, or even if America would emerge the victor. In contemplating America after the war few citizens longed for a new world order; instead, most yearned for a return to the safety and familiarity of prewar life.

But World War II brought momentous change. It redressed boundaries, it reshaped landscapes and cities, it reformed identities and allegiances, and it gave new meaning to the horrors of death and destruction. The years 1941–45 were an intensely emotional time for Americans. Heightened feelings of patriotism and pride were tempered by periods of anxiety, fear, frustration, tension, strife, and grief. Although America escaped the devastation that much of Europe and Asia suffered, the nation's most fundamental social institutions—family, home, neighborhood, and workplace—were nevertheless transformed by the war effort. The exhibition *Chicago Goes to War, 1941–45* and this accompanying catalogue tell the story of one city's attempt to cope with the war and the changes it brought.

The homefront has received only modest attention from historians. The fiftieth anniversary of the attack on Pearl Harbor has inspired a number of new publications and exhibitions that explore homefront life in greater detail. But conspicuously lacking in the scholarship are case studies of the impact of the war on America's major urban-industrial centers.

Chicago is an ideal city for such a study because its homefront experience was in many ways typical and in other ways unique in the nation. Chicagoans, like Americans everywhere, participated in government-sanctioned domestic programs and activities that tended to homogenize the homefront experience throughout the nation—everything from victory gardens to mock bombings to war bond drives to collecting scrap. But as the nation's transportation hub, Chicago was uniquely suited to be the central handling point of military personnel and materiel. In addition, its diverse manufacturing capability, coupled with its crossroads position, gave the city a major role in war production. Chicago was also unique in its efforts to promote interracial understanding and cooperation among its citizens at a time when other major cities were plagued by race riots. And Chicagoans welcomed the resettlement of more than twenty thousand Japanese-Americans released from internment camps in the West, more than in any other city in the nation. For students of city history, an examination of Chicago's homefront experience promises to yield a richly detailed portrait of urban life during war.

But museum exhibitions are more than scholarship directed to a handful of specialists in the field; they are also one of the few, and among the more stimulating, avenues that bring history to the public. *Chicago Goes to War, 1941–45* is part of an ambitious series of exhibitions organized by the Chicago Historical

Society under the title, "Prologue for a New Century." Inaugurated in 1990 with the exhibition *A City Comes of Age: Chicago in the 1890s*, this series has two major goals: first, to work in partnership with academic historians to make the most current scholarship accessible to larger audiences; and second, to help the public understand our own time through an interpretation of the past.

Perry R. Duis, associate professor of history at the University of Illinois at Chicago, first proposed this exhibition to the Society's Staff Exhibition Committee in August 1989. The committee accepted the proposal as an ideal topic for a second biennial exhibition and asked Scott La France, associate curator of the Society's Charles F. Murphy Architectural Study Center, to share curatorial duties with Perry. Perry and Scott formed a partnership that creatively balanced each other's strengths. Perry brought the perspective of an urban historian and his vast knowledge of Chicago's history to the project, while Scott drew on his understanding as a museum curator of the power and the language of artifacts to convey historical ideas.

Creating a three-dimensional interpretation of the homefront experience with public appeal proved to be a bigger challenge. The Society has traditionally drawn heavily from its own collections for its exhibitions, but the curators discovered early that the museum did not have the necessary artifacts to tell the story. In September 1990, the Society issued a public call to all Chicagoans for homefront artifacts, the first exhibition-related collection drive in the institution's history. The response was overwhelming. Generous donations and loans of family mementos, business records, and industrial products and equipment filled our storage area and led to discoveries of other artifacts that might have gone unnoticed.

Happily, almost every artifact came with a story. Homefront memories remain vivid for the generation of Chicagoans who lived during the World War II years. Their willingness to share their remembrances with us, and the curators' eagerness to incorporate them into the exhibition represents a new kind of partnership for the Society. This approach to exhibitions also reflects the Society's commitment to share with all Chicagoans the authority to tell the history of their city. Indeed, in our role as historian of the city, the Society realizes that Chicago's history can only be told by working in close concert with the city's diverse communities. Thanks to Scott and Perry, the story of Chicagoans going to war has been greatly enriched by a communitywide effort involving more than five hundred individuals, businesses, groups, and associations.

An enterprise as large as this one requires a virtual army of support staff. It is my privilege to acknowledge a number of them whose special contributions and extraordinary efforts helped make this exhibition possible. In addition to thanking Perry Duis and Scott La France for expertly guiding their curatorial vision to completion, I owe thanks to Ellsworth H. Brown, the Society's president and director, for challenging us to think more creatively. Susan Page Tillett, director of curatorial affairs, passed on to me the baton of project director for this exhibition and provided an exemplary model; for her help in preparing me for the travails of the job, I am truly grateful. Joanne Grossman and Anna Holian took on the major responsibility of coordinating much of the day-to-day curatorial work, which they carried out with intelligence, professionalism, and good cheer. Andrew Leo and Michael Biddle stretched the limits of conventional exhibition design with their bold and inventive solutions, and Ted Gibbs provided exceptional graphic and label designs. Myron Freedman and Walter Reinhardt managed the difficult jobs of fabrication and installation with finesse and efficiency. Rosemary Adams coordinated all aspects of the exhibition's publications with decisiveness and dispatch, and her editorial acumen is evident in each page of this catalogue and in every label. She was ably assisted by Patricia Bereck Weikersheimer. Bill Van Nimwegen's lively and inviting catalogue design conveys the spirit of the war years. Michael Sarna managed the shipping and registration of artifacts with aplomb. Lynn McRainey, Amina Dickerson, Bonnie Garmisa, and Eva Olson created compelling educational and public programming. Mary Janzen wrote successful grant applications to the National Endowment for the Humanities and the Illinois Humanities Council. Pat Kremer coordinated the public relations campaign. Special thanks to Gary Mitchiner and his associates at Hal Riney & Partners, Inc. for their pro bono work on the advertising campaign. John Alderson switched his camera for earphones to create the exhibition's sound collage. Don Renaud and Robert Parker tracked the budget. Consultants Charles Branham, Susan Hartmann, James Hirabayashi, and Richard Polenberg reviewed our exhibition proposal and label text and offered useful advice and encouragement.

Several of the staff listed above were part of the exhibition team, a core group of staff members who planned, scheduled, reviewed, judged, and debated every aspect of the exhibition. For their exceptional commitment to this project, I am especially grateful to Rosemary Adams, Mike Biddle, Perry Duis, Joanne Grossman, Anna Holian, Scott La France, Andy Leo, Lynn McRainey, and Mike Sarna. Their participation at this level made my job as project director not only easier, but truly pleasurable.

Many members of the curatorial staff offered encouragement and advice and combed through their collections for appropriate artifacts. Claire Cass of the Prints and Photographs Collection and Susan Samek of the Costume Collection were especially helpful. Thanks also to Louise Brownell, Emily Clark, Bob Goler, and Ralph Pugh. Carol Turchan and Terri Edwards were joined by Nancy Rubins, Chris Del Re, and Rick Strilky in conserving the artifacts. John Alderson and Jay Crawford maintained the highest standards of quality in their photography despite a deluge of orders.

Trustee Richard M. Jaffee chaired an advisory committee of fellow trustees and business leaders to secure funding for the exhibition. Under Mr. Jaffee's leadership, and with the assistance of Barbara Reed, Marc Hilton, Donald McFerren, and Joe Sopcich of the development staff, the exhibition received generous support. The Robert R. McCormick Tribune Foundation provided major underwriting, and I am especially grateful to General Neil Creighton, USA (Ret.), president of the foundation, for his early support and encouragement. The National Endowment for the Humanities has been an unstinting supporter of many of the Society's past exhibitions. I was deeply gratified to receive, once again, major assistance from them in the form of planning and implementation grants. Additional funding came from Oil-Dri Corporation of America, thanks to Richard Jaffee; MIDCON Corporation, GATX Corporation, the Illinois Humanities Council, and the Pepsi-Cola Company.

In an address before the American Booksellers Association in April 1942, President Franklin Delano Roosevelt told his audience, "No man and no force can abolish memory." In creating this exhibition we have strived not only to recognize the value of everyday Chicagoan's memories as historical perspective, but to tap into the power of those memories as bridges from the past to the present.

Introduction

This is the story of what happened in Chicago between December 7, 1941, the day the Japanese attacked Pearl Harbor, and August 14, 1945, when hundreds of thousands of Chicagoans poured into the streets to celebrate V-J Day. While the city was part of a nation at war, this book focuses on what happened in Chicago, because it is an effort to find meaning for the event in the context of the urban transformation of one city. It is not the story of what happened on the battlefronts of Europe and the Pacific, though without the sacrifices made there, the story of the homefront would have taken a very different turn. At the same time, had Chicagoans and millions of other Americans not made the domestic sacrifices described in the following pages, the military effort surely would have failed. Each half of the war story depends on the other. Because what happened on the homefront relates to what happened on the battlefields, a chronology of the events of the war can be found on page 134 of this book.

Although the attack on Pearl Harbor shocked the nation, American entry into the war surprised few people. The debate over America's role in the world took on new meaning when war clouds began to gather in the late-1930s. The growing problem of Japanese expansionism had captured the nation's attention first. Tens of thousands of Chicagoans heard President Franklin D. Roosevelt himself warn of impending trouble when he came to town to dedicate the Outer Drive Bridge on October 5, 1937. In what was quickly labeled the "quarantine speech," Roosevelt suggested that, like a disease, the spread of Japan might have to be checked by other nations.[1]

Chicagoans, however, were more concerned with events in Europe, perhaps because those events seemed to have a more immediate impact on the United States. When the shooting war broke out in Europe in 1939, American factories soon became shadow combatants through lend-lease arrangements. In 1940 Congress enacted the first peacetime conscription, and the prospect of direct military involvement became even more immediate.[2]

Chicago was the scene of a rancorous debate over American involvement in the war that attracted worldwide attention. On one side stood Col. Robert R. McCormick and the *Chicago Tribune*. McCormick represented a viewpoint widely held in the Midwest: direct American involvement in the war in Europe would be a mistake. The flattened American economy meant that the nation could not afford to be a world policeman. Nor did the United States have a mandate to preserve a British-dominated "Atlantic civilization," a concept McCormick rejected because he felt that American culture was unique, far removed from European culture. In editorials and slanted news stories, the *Tribune* condemned America's foreign policy as one Roosevelt blunder after another. McCormick helped catalyze the creation of a national isolationist movement called the America First Committee.[3]

1

McCormick met his match in Col. Frank Knox, the publisher of the *Daily News*. Knox's editorials blasted and belittled "Col. McCosmick" for failing to understand that modern communications and air transportation, as well as the emergence of global business, had drawn America into a world community, whether it wanted to be there or not. Ignoring events abroad was the height of irresponsibility. The rise of the Nazis threatened Western civilization itself, and the loss of France, England, and the rest of Western Europe would mean the destruction of America's roots. Supporters of interventionism, including the Committee to Defend America by Aiding the Allies, emphasized a second threat: if the Nazis succeeded in conquering England and Greenland, even Chicago might be vulnerable to attack one day. So strong was this opinion that the *Daily News* loaned the use of its presses to Marshall Field III, scion of the department store family, to help launch a newspaper to provide direct morning competition to the *Tribune*. The first issue of the *Chicago Sun* appeared on December 4, 1941.[4] Four days later, the United States was at war.

✪　✪　✪　✪　✪　✪

Several themes reappear throughout the story of homefront Chicago. One is the intricate interplay between surplus and shortage, a wobbling imbalance of the normal economic life that grew out of the impact of billions of dollars in defense contracts on the city's industries. During the war, more jobs were held by more Chicagoans in more new factories that paid more money than at any other time in the twentieth century. Moreover, the abundance of money was in the hands of the many, not the few. Amidst this abundance, however, there seemed to be shortages of almost everything, including housing, consumer goods, factory workers, and raw materials.

There was also a sense of a compressed time. The years 1941 through 1945 seemed to cram eventful change into a short time frame. This compression of time was personal as well as national. The sweep of world events forced individuals to make instant decisions in their private lives. The rushed pace of everything even suggests a scarcity of time. These shortages, in turn, helped stimulate innovation, substitution, and the quiet crime of black markets.

This story is told thematically, not chronologically, because there is a logical outward-expanding pattern to the story of wartime Chicago. It begins in the home. Whether an apartment or a house, humble or grand, here families shared their personal views of the world. Here families welcomed their loved ones home from war or mourned their deaths. The war, however, brought a wholesale invasion of that sense of family privacy. In the neighborhood, affairs were more public, but they were still largely governed by relationships with people whose names were known. Because so much of the city's social life was already organized through the neighborhoods, they became the basic building block of the organized homefront effort. The industrial plant drew men and women from their homes and neighborhoods into a larger sphere. The war transformed the familiar factory into a work community—indoctrinated, efficient, and secure. Finally, the last chapter focuses on a highly public aspect of the war, Chicago's Loop, which served as a crossroads for the city itself as well as for the entire nation. The most public events of the war occurred in the place where the city's social, economic, and political life was focused: downtown. Chicago's national role as the place where Americans changed trains took on new meaning during the war.

Many people who lived through World War II remember the sense of unified purpose and the patriotism of those years. The painful divisiveness that followed, especially during the 1960s, makes the 1940s seem like a utopia lost. But the reality of homefront Chicago was quite different. Optimism and pessimism ebbed and flowed during those four years. Enthusiasm turned to tolerance, then tedium and even resistance.

Although today we know what happened, those living through the war did not. No one knew if or when the Allies would triumph. No one knew what the impact of government controls and regulations would be. No families knew if their loved ones would return home safely. The wisdom of half a century's hindsight not only allows us to know what happened, but also to interpret connections between seemingly unrelated events.

The war permeated everyday life on the homefront. Patriotic symbols were ubiquitous, announcing the support and loyalty of individuals and families. Window cards, service flags, and even jewelry displayed "V" for victory as well as service stars, each of which represented a family member in the military.

THIS IS A **V** HOME

 WARDEN

The Household War

The story of Chicago during World War II properly begins at home. The home was the place of most personal contact with the faraway conflict. Here the draft notice was received, the son or daughter was welcomed home, or the dreaded casualty telegram arrived. The stateside impact of the war struck home first. Every Chicago household coped with shortages, substitutions, and rationing, as the nation underwent the massive reallocation of resources necessary to fight the enemy.

The war touched every room in the house. Would there be new furniture for the living room or sheets for the bedroom? Would bathroom soap or razor blades be rationed? What food would be on the dining room table or in the refrigerator? It was ironic that while there was nothing as individualized as each of the hundreds of thousands of households in the nation's second largest city, there was perhaps no experience as universal as that of the frustrated consumer.

Families New and Old

At its most invasive, World War II violated the traditional ideal that privacy and independence strengthened family ties. In this perfect world, a man worked to support his family; his wife remained home to care for the children. Home was a protective place where the family determined what information, ideas, people, and materials entered from the outside. Obviously, the ideal of controlled isolation was seldom completely achieved, even in peacetime. The media, peer groups, school—

dozens of factors compromised the ideal family living space. But World War II involved an especially intense violation of this model world of the family.

The war bride is perhaps the most enduring symbol of the changes in traditional family life. The first emotional responses to Pearl Harbor spawned a sudden increase in the number of marriages. There had already been an expansion of new households as the new prosperity generated by the late 1930s arms buildup eased the economic restraints of the depression and more Chicagoans could afford to marry. But during the days immediately following December 7, the Cook County clerk issued marriage licenses at twice the usual rate. The compression of time that accompanied the nation's hectic plunge into a shooting war forced Americans to make instant decisions on the personal, as well as the national, level. Some couples had planned to

Toys and games took on a contemporary military and political focus during the war. The traditional conflict between good and evil in children's play was represented by the Allies and the Axis.

Reach Your Boy
OVERSEAS
by
V-mail
the letters
that travel on film
EASY TO USE
SUREST —
FASTEST —
and **MOST**
PATRIOTIC

V···· Your Stationer and Post Office have
—MAIL LETTER FORMS

Many families separated were by the war and keeping in touch through letters was vital to maintaining morale both on the home front and on the battlefront. The government instituted V-mail as a way to decrease the amount of valuable cargo space taken up by mail.

wed later; others enjoyed what the sociologists labeled "furlough romances," bonds created between people who had known each other a short time.[1]

Nothing remained the same. Traditions such as a service in the bride's hometown and formal wedding invitations gave way to quick ceremonies that were often arranged as a package by a department store.[2] The departure of a new husband to the military delayed the creation of a traditional household, causing more problems. A psychiatric consultant for the Chicago-based Association for Family Living recommended that a childless wife become roommates with another "war widow," get a job, and begin planning for anticipated postwar adjustment problems. Many young war brides set up temporary housekeeping in tiny apartments; others ignored the advice of experts and moved back home with their parents.[3]

After the rush of instant decisions came the wait and the worry and the loneliness. The press emphasized the loneliness that accompanied separation, a condition that *Daily News* columnist Emery Hutchinson called the "new plague." Its victims sought refuge in bars. "They're just trying to fill the time, I suppose," commented one priest, "But they are developing habits that their husbands wouldn't like to think of them having."[4] Dramatic headlines told of one result of it: "Hunt a 'Why?' After Suicide of Girl Nurse" and "Wife of a Soldier Leaves Party, Ends Life With a Revolver."[5] Most women simply coped, sometimes with the help of clubs formed for servicemen's wives. Members met frequently to assemble packages and provide emotional support for each other.[6] Similar organizations aided the mothers of military personnel.[7]

Families were not completely cut off from loved ones in the military. As it had in every war before, the post office was a pipeline of news and affection. Families supplied what the military could not: a bit of home. The quantity of packages and letters, however, soon burdened supply lines. Instead of restricting letters, which might have injured morale, the government turned to technology. On June 20, 1942, it instituted V-mail. Senders squeezed their messages on small sheets, which the Army Signal Corps photographed on 16-mm microfilm reels at the rate of twenty-five hundred letters per hour. The writing space on the special forms was cramped, however, and delivery seemed slow. V-mail also made it easier for censors to eliminate so-called "family codes," by which personnel tried to inform the folks back home of their whereabouts. Military intelligence experts feared that such innocent messages might provide enemy espionage agents with classified information about troop movements.[8]

Personal packages posed another problem. Shipments of food, books, and photographs flowed to the troops in such large quantities that in January 1943 new regulations limited what could be sent to articles specifically requested by service personnel and approved by their battalion commanders. In July 1944, the *Tribune* solved part of the problem when it began reproducing the photographs of mothers and infants on V-mail forms so that fathers could see the children born since they had left home.[9] Information from home also came in the form of the media. The *Tribune* sent a special reduced-format edition to servicemen abroad, as did *Time* and *Newsweek*, while the *Daily News* published a weekly box summary of local events that was meant to be clipped by families and sent overseas.[10]

The war threatened the traditional home in an even more basic way through its eroding impact on many marriages. The wave of wartime wedlock, which was concentrated between

December 1941 and late 1943, finally subsided when the number of furloughs declined and larger numbers of prospective husbands went abroad. By then, the focus of popular discussion began to shift to the question of how long these military marriages would last. "Total war changes people and things, and John and Jane will never be the same again," noted *Tribune* writer Lloyd Wendt. "Whether they can take up normal life together as man and wife when the show is over will depend upon whether the values they share are far more stable than mere romantic infatuation, hero worship, physical attraction, and the excitement of the moment."

Sociologists and social workers observed that such hasty unions during World War I had led to an extraordinary divorce rate during the early 1920s and predicted that it was likely to happen again. Wendt summarized one part of the problem: "In wartime not only is the pattern of family living disrupted but individual sex urge is released. . . . Men and women are in uniform, almost everyone moves out of his customary orbit and at least pretends to be some one different. This change and posing . . . release extra sexual impulse. . . . The greatest manifestation of the impulse is outside marriage."[11]

Above, some soldiers illustrated their V-mail letters with drawings that humorously conveyed the loneliness they felt.

"I've found the job where I fit best!"

FIND YOUR WAR JOB
In Industry – Agriculture – Business

Above, the government urged women to find jobs in defense industries. During the war middle-class married women entered the work force in unprecedented numbers, often performing work traditionally done only by men.

The divorce rate increased only moderately during the first half of the war, in part because so many men remained overseas, while their wives were unwilling to give up their family allotments. As men began returning in the fall of 1944, the divorce rate reached peak levels, but the predicted doom of the postwar family caused the greatest concern. Gloomy prognostication became a cottage industry for sociologists and newspaper writers. They saw a nation increasingly populated by people whose ties with home had been broken by the wartime experience, as well as an era that tolerated greater promiscuity. Sociologists also worried about money in the hands of working women and how it might increase the divorce rate. Money in the bank meant the means to hire a lawyer.[12]

Women Go to Work

The lives of most Chicago families did not change dramatically during the early months of the conflict. Most husbands remained stateside, working extra hours and bringing home larger paychecks, and most women were not employed outside of the home. Ultimately, however, the growing demand for workers to manufacture the implements of war—and to fill the jobs of others who changed jobs—altered everything. By the end of 1943, over 130,000 Chicago families saw their wives and mothers enter the work force.

The creation of Chicago's "Rosie the Riveter" came in stages. Shaping the social impact of World War II on Chicago was primarily the fluctuation in the demand for female labor. Initially, some city officials and plant managers were either indifferent or openly hostile to the idea of women, especially mothers, working outside of the home. Interest grew, however, during the months following Pearl Harbor. Early in 1942, for instance, the state department of labor initiated a study to determine what job opportunities awaited women graduating from high school. Companies were then highly selective, with strict maximum age limits—usually thirty—and many, such as Studebaker, refused to hire women for non-office work.[13] This reluctance to hire women also reflected the low demand for workers early in the war. Chicago did not obtain many major defense contracts in areas such as the aircraft industry until well into 1942. Much of that work and the intense demand for workers had to await the construction of new defense plants. Meanwhile, the pool of unemployed men continued to fill most labor needs.[14]

By the beginning of 1943, however, employers intensified their calls for female workers; by the end of that year, these appeals were increasingly desperate. Local industrial buildup expanded much more rapidly than anyone could have predicted. An extreme need to enlarge the labor pool from within the present population resulted, and the largest potential source was Chicago's women. Initially, the War Manpower Commission, the federal agency responsible for making the most efficient use of the American work force, was selective. In May 1943 it appealed to single women and married women who were either childless or had no youngsters under the age of fourteen. By the following September, the commission had decided that Chicago was heading toward an extreme labor shortage, which meant severe limits on new war contracts and the imposition of a mandatory and universal forty-eight-hour workweek. Industrialists and civic leaders, who were beginning to see women as the region's saviors, began launching recruiting drives.[15]

By the early months of 1944, low-pressure recruiting efforts yielded to more aggressive pleas that insinuated that women who did not work were unpatriotic. Chicago Mayor Edward J. Kelly issued such an appeal early in February, the first "women only" recruiting call in the city's labor history. Mary Anderson, a former Chicagoan and director of the Women's Bureau of the U.S. Department of Labor, answered such appeals by saying that the labor shortage was "not the fault of women." By then, 43 percent of Chicago-area women held jobs outside of the home, seventy-five thousand of them during 1943. By June 1944 some 300,000 were at work, a 110 percent increase since mid-1940. But even then, corporations desperate to secure new labor contracts carried recruiting to a level that infringed on the privacy of women. The Rauland Corporation, makers of radar and communications equipment, and eight North Chicago firms dispatched teams of employees to recruit women door-to-door six days a week. On their first day, the North Chicago group made 892 calls, talked to 604 women, and signed eighty-five new employees.[16]

Women worked for a variety of reasons. Some were lonely; others did it out of patriotism. But most needed the money to support themselves, to pay off debts, to improve their families' standard of living, or to put aside some funds for the postwar economic depression that so many experts predicted. Whatever the motivation, women workers and their families reorganized their lives to accommodate women's new roles.

The press never tired of recounting the stories of superachievers. The *Daily News* told of the Tansor family of North Milwaukee Avenue. Etta, a wife, mother, and war worker, arose six evenings a week at 9:30 P.M. to prepare for the 11:30 P.M. shift at the Rock-Ola plant at Chicago and Kedzie avenues. For the next eight hours she supervised a "battery of girl machinists," arriving home a little after 8 A.M. By then her husband, Lawrence, had already fed their three children and was preparing to leave for his job as a Chicago and North Western Railroad engineer. Etta spent the rest of the morning housecleaning and shopping. At 2 P.M. her evening's rest began. There were tens of thousands of unheralded families who were much like the Tansors.

Above, "Victory" jewelry. Left, a female worker's security badge.

Childhood, Adolescence, and the War

During World War II, birthrates climbed to their highest since the 1920s. Undoubtedly, some pregnancies were related to draft deferments granted to fathers—at least until those ended on December 5, 1943. But most were prompted by the return to prosperity that had begun during the two years before Pearl Harbor. Many couples, who had deferred having families because of the depression, were determined to have children before they became too old. As late as 1944, one-third of all live births were to women in their thirties having their first child.[17]

The fact that parents were more mature did not allay society's uneasiness about what was happening to the traditional home and its effect on children. Experts agreed that youngsters of all ages needed protective and nurturing homes, the privacy and sanctity of which were compromised by the war. Each age group faced unique problems, which generated numerous reports, congressional hearings, conferences, and newspaper exposes and editorials. Most people agreed that the younger children needed to be sheltered from fear, but not necessarily from the war. Most youngsters heard the war news, interpreting it in personal ways. One wartime youngster later recalled confusing "germs" and "Germans," so that she tried to wash "the enemy" away with soap and vigorous scrubbing.[18] India Moffett, who

Above, Axis leaders, such as Japan's Emperor Hirohito, were vilified in unlikely places. This target is from a Riverview Park game. Below, toys based on contemporary military themes, such as these "Sailor Bob" and "Our WAVE Patsy" paper dolls, were common during the war.

wrote the *Tribune*'s "Women in War Work" column, described a visit to the pet counter of a Loop department store. There, she found children agonizing over the rules that excluded dogs and cats from bomb shelters. "Gee, the bombs'll have to get me if my pooch can't get in with me," lamented one youngster.[19]

Inevitably the war became part of childhood play. Commercial toy makers had begun incorporating military themes even before Pearl Harbor. Electric trains pulled cars with searchlights and antiaircraft guns. There was Mickey Mouse in an airplane, as well as a myriad of tanks and armored trucks. Another toy featured a dive-bomber that slid down a wire and released its payload over a target and a fully equipped naval base kit; a child could thus reenact Pearl Harbor. Shortages of some raw materials also forced changes in toys available. The toy soldiers of 1941 were made of wood or cardboard instead of tin or lead. Children were urged to use scraps in craft projects to make the family's presents. Model-airplane makers sold kits for every type of military and civilian plane, Allied and Axis alike.[20] The federal government encouraged model-building of all types both because it helped build morale among youth and taught basic principles of aviation for future fliers.

Not everyone approved of the way in which war had become part of childhood. Advice columnists echoed the concerns expressed by psychologists that the war overstimulated children, who, in the words of Angelo Patri of the *Daily News*, "play war games, attack, defend, shoot and fall dead every spare hour. . . . They listen to radio programs that further excite them, they go to movies and get more of the same." Patri recommended that children become involved with sports, gardening, household chores, and pets to distract them from the war.[21]

Homes Away From Home

The movement of women into the work force made it even more difficult to shelter children, especially the younger ones, from the outside world. The press chronicled the perils of latchkey children who were left home alone to fend for themselves. By July 1942, before the heaviest recruiting of female war workers even began, authorities had already uncovered incidences of toddlers locked up all day in trailers or cars parked in defense plant parking lots. One survey of grade-school children by the Juvenile Protective Association revealed at least forty-five hundred youngsters left without supervision. The problem touched all parts of the city, not just working-class neighborhoods. [22]

A part-time substitute for the family that moved the child out of the private home and into the neighborhood or larger community was needed. The question was who would provide it. Samuel Cardinal Stritch, the archbishop of Chicago, warned against too much state intervention, noting that in fascist countries, government childcare had undermined churches and private groups. His own survey of Roman Catholic parishes in the Chicago archdiocese revealed that of eight thousand war-worker mothers, only 719 were unable to provide adequately for their children. Parish members came forward, and, according to Stritch, "[t]heir problem was at once cared for."[23]

On occasion, retired neighbors watched preschoolers; they welcomed the extra income as a supplement to Social Security payments. "It gives us the feeling that we are doing something to help win the fight," noted one old couple who lived near Oakenwald School on the South Side.[24] Some industrial plants also provided day-care facilities. Republic Drill and Douglas Aircraft both opened on-site day-care facilities to minimize commuting times for their widely scattered employees.[25]

Many parents, however, had to rely on publicly funded centers. Most of the forty facilities operating in 1942 had been started by the depression-era Works Progress Administration (WPA) and continued after Pearl Harbor. The termination of all federal relief projects in 1943 brought a shift to new funding from Washington and new management locally. The Chicago Public School System took up part of the slack, as did such private neighborhood groups as the Hyde Park Nursery Association, the North Avenue Day Nursery, and several social settlement houses.[26] By 1945 there were 117 facilities, forty-eight of them operated by the Board of Education. But many were short-staffed, in part no doubt because would-be "part-time mothers" were intimidated by the Office of Civilian Defense (OCD) requirement of a seventy-eight-hour training course.

During the last six months of the war parents complained that the centers' hours were too short, and that many were closed on Saturday, which was a normal workday for many parents. In addition, sixty-nine of the 117 centers violated fire and health codes. Center operators, in turn, complained that parents often dropped off children who had not had breakfast or were ill, and that many of those

Peter Johnsen

I was three when the war broke out. . . . It was frightening. It was very real. And I think what convinced me of the reality of it was watching. Because children are tuned into . . . the adults around them. They're your lightning rods. And the changes that were going on with the adults was just incredible. . . . I didn't see much of my father throughout the whole war because he was at work. He came home, I was in bed. I got up and went to school. He got up and went to work before I came back. You know, I saw him on weekends! He worked on the holidays; I didn't even see him on Christmas.

I think it was every boy's duty to be able to spot airplanes. You really got a dose of it, because it was on the back of your cereal boxes facing you in the morning . . . how to spot them! And you were supposed to listen as well, and I'll tell you that today I still stop when I hear a propellor-driven airplane, and I immediately do this! [he snaps his fingers and looks up] There's no fear any more, but the reaction is still there!

Schools were involved with many aspects of the war. Children at the St. Augustine school in the Back of the Yards neighborhood crowd around the army jeep they raised money for.

the money to help with family living expenses in the absence of a father. Others, who had spent most of their younger years facing the deprivations of the depression, were tempted by the lure of money. As the city grappled with a general labor shortage, many adult workers in low-paying occupations moved up the scale, leaving a shortage of bowling alley pinsetters, stock boys in stores, and gasoline station attendants. Thousands of youngsters took summer jobs and never returned to school. Each autumn through the war years the press reported a decline in high school enrollment, which tumbled from 141,000 in 1939 to 119,000 three years later. Some of the decline resulted from a sharp drop in the depression-era birthrate, but dropouts were the main problem. School officials tried to lure teenagers back to the classroom by reducing the homework load and concentrating school hours into half-day sessions, but most of the losses were permanent.[28]

The question of when adulthood properly began contained another question: what degree of personal freedom should accompany the plunge into the grown-up world? Under the pressure of wartime conformity, anything that seemed to divert attention away from whole-hearted devotion to patriotic endeavor was labeled as dangerous. Experts who studied Chicago youth during the war were dismayed at what they viewed as a defiant attitude among teenagers. The anonymity of the city only exacerbated the question of freedom in the plunge into quasi adulthood for teenagers. Public transit and automobiles took other youngsters far from the surveillance of family and neighbors. When some parents began taking public transit to work, their children took the cars for wild rides to many of the same "joints" their parents had frequented during Prohibition. Strips on Harlem Avenue, just north of North Avenue, and another on

who used the government-subsidized, low-fee public centers could easily afford private ones. Summertime school closing created another problem, which was only partially solved by special programs operated by the Chicago Park District. [27]

Many experts were also increasingly concerned that the war was bringing childhood and adolescence to a premature end. The workplace beckoned. Illinois led the nation in violations of child labor laws, which forbade employment for youths under the age of fourteen and required a work certificate for fourteen- and fifteen-year-olds. Tens of thousands of youngsters entered the adult work force before high school graduation. Some needed

Skokie Road acquired reputations for catering to carloads of underage drinkers.[29]

The experts were particularly concerned about teenage girls who necked in darkened theater balconies, hung around on street corners, and headed to the Loop each night.[30] Grant Park became the central rendezvous where they met military personnel, who were also in search of a place free from the peering eyes of authority. "Most of them are uniform crazy and sexually promiscuous," grumbled Antoinette Quinn, one of a dozen police officers who patrolled the Loop every night.[31] Some were runaways, both local and out-of-town. The press agonized over the causes and consequences of wartime necking. Some girls said that "romance is passing us by, and we want a good time before all the young men are taken away." Others cited their own version of "patriotism," claiming that "the boys may be leaving for the front soon, and they're entitled to all the fun we can give them."

Teenage boys, many of whom were only months away from probable draft and the danger of the battlefield, echoed this "have our fling" mentality. The press often ran features on what high school boys thought of their futures. While the interviewees were uniformly patriotic, writers described "a general nervousness" in the boys, which led to "adolescent maladjustment" and a permissive attitude on the part of the parents. "This is wartime, isn't it?" replied one teenager. "We're the ones who will have to do the fighting, and we might as well have our fun while we can."[32]

Whatever the explanation for this youthful defiance, authorities blamed it on the deterioration of the family. Juvenile experts complained that parents who drank, argued in front of their children, evaded rationing regulations, and otherwise set poor examples were the root of "90 percent of the problem."[33] Police captain Thomas Duffy said that parents "are the ones who are mostly to blame because in many cases both of them are out chasing the almighty dollar. They neglect their children's religious training and allow them too much money to spend."[34] That money too often ended up paying for liquor or sex.[35] Others blamed the problem on working women. The issue of delinquency attracted the greatest concern at about the same time the major industrial recruiting drives for women began. Still others disagreed that the "youth problem" constituted a major "wave" caused by the war.

Whatever the causes, solutions were elusive. Unlike other homefront-related situations, the youth problem could not be corrected with a government directive. By early 1944, experts had begun making some suggestions, ranging from an expansion of wholesome clubs and teen centers to a revival of the curfew and new juvenile court facilities.[36]

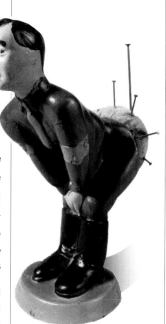

Above, this Hitler skunk and pin cushion caricature the German leader. Left, the walls of a boy's bedroom illustrate his interest in bombers and pinup girls.

This hairpin package illustrates the pervasiveness of the war. Women were encouraged to reuse the pins because of the shortage of metals.

Under Seige: The Chicago Consumer

With the war came the return of prosperity to many Americans. Unemployment fell to record low levels, reaching about 1 percent in 1944, and defense industry checks were much larger than most people had seen in over a decade.[37] Most consumers earned something, often more than what was needed for basic living expenses. In addition to buying defense bonds, thousands of Chicago families paid past-due mortgages and other debts. Some of what was left over often went into a bank or savings and loan account. Prosperity itself, along with federal deposit insurance, removed much of the fear of runs on banks.[38] There was always something left to spend, and many Chicagoans joined fellow Americans in feeling that the deprivation suffered during the depression entitled them to a little self-indulgence. Department store sales soared in 1941 and hit record levels during the 1941 Christmas season.[39] Shoppers, fearful of wartime restrictions, bought everything they could and paid cash.

The new prosperity made it even more difficult to cope with the impact of dwindling supplies of labor and raw materials available for the production of consumer goods. There were shortages of almost everything. Tires disappeared from store shelves first. Early in 1942 the Office of Price Administration (OPA) virtually halted the production of nearly six hundred types of consumer goods that were made in part with some raw material in short supply. This affected everything from hair dryers to bobby pins, from hot water bottles to babies' rubber pants, from vacuum cleaners to bicycles. Normal consumer demand would have speedily depleted the warehouse supplies, but panic buying did the job quickly. [40]

Homeowners could not buy window screens or caulking. Directives cut phonographic record production by 30 percent, and, after March 1942, there were no new jukeboxes on which to play them. The shortages also reduced the consumer's choice of items. Because of restrictions on alcohol, wax, glycerine, and metal containers, women could not buy lipstick. Housepaint supplies declined because American linseed production had been diverted to oleomargarine for the Soviet Union.

Insufficient supplies of some goods created a dilemma for government planners. Servicemen's centers relied on the benevolence of the public for equipment donations. They suffered the same problem that every family faced: burned-out radio tubes that could not be replaced. Public grumbling, along with the realization that families with broken radios could not hear civilian defense orders or President Roosevelt's fireside chats, forced an easing of tube manufacturing restrictions in April 1943.[41]

The shortages led to a series of substitutions. Where possible, wood supplanted metal, even as occasional replacements for car bumpers, where paint had routinely taken the place of chrome. Sears, Roebuck offered a line of upholstered furniture with wooden springs. The war also introduced many consumers to plastics. Electrical sockets and switches used metal only in the parts that carried the current. Flashlight producers switched over from aluminum, rubber, nickel, or chromium to plastic. The development of nylon also eased the demand for silk stockings, supplies of which had been appropriated for use in parachute cord. The demand for genuine silk stockings became so intense that one Chicago department store refused a chance to buy fifty thousand pairs, fearing that its store would be wrecked by the surging mob of buyers. [42]

The shortages also affected the style of everyday items, especially clothing. Federal officials realized that domestic garment manufacture had to continue because wardrobes eventually wore out, but edicts shortened women's hemlines and reduced the amount of unnecessary trim and patch pockets, which wasted cloth. Women's garments were often tied at the sides to eliminate zippers, which were deemed a waste of metal. Styles became conservative because women would have to keep garments longer. Newspaper columns advised how new accessories could revitalize an aging wardrobe.[43] Men faced similar clothing restrictions. Two-trouser suits, pants pleats, patch pockets, and vests disappeared by order of the OPA. During the last hours before the April 1, 1942, deadline, tailors were swamped with orders for new pants with cuffs.[44]

The ephemeral nature of clothing made it especially susceptible to restrictions on style, but other manufacturers also saw innovation temporarily halted. The American Furniture Mart, for instance, usually saw over five hundred new items introduced each year; during the war years it averaged five per year. The changes that did take place were dictated by external forces. Metal furniture, which had become popular during the late 1930s, disappeared from the market as manufacturers returned to wood. Some makers replaced nails with wooden pegs; other companies turned to wooden replacements for traditionally metal items such as bicycle pedals and toys. Furniture-makers hoped to profit from a new market they envisioned for scaled-down pieces for the smaller rooms of the housing constructed for defense workers, but that market largely failed to materialize. Most consumers either kept their old pieces or bought older ones. Antiques and slipcovers made a comeback.[45]

Wartime catalogs issued by Chicago's giant mail-order houses reflected the shortages faced by consumers. Not only did these retailers promise to comply with price guidelines, but they also included forms for collecting ration stamps. Product availability directly affected what was in their "wish books." Like all retailers, Montgomery Wards and Sears dropped many lines of merchandise, liquidating remaining stocks through stores. The catalogs shrank in size and most also contained page after page of goods marked with asterisks that indicated items out of stock because of government restrictions. Offerings of soft goods, especially "practical clothing," expanded to fill the void. The war made its impact felt everywhere, with new listings of vitamins, page after page of slacks and foundation garments for women in the industrial work force, knit work shirts for men (tighter fit meant less likelihood of accidental entanglement in machinery), and unpainted furniture. A more ominous reflection of the war was a new line of merchandise introduced by Sears in its spring-summer 1944 catalog: tombstones.[46]

Women who worked in defense factories were encouraged to wear practical clothing for safety. They were assured that they could retain their femininity despite the more masculine, utilitarian style of such clothing.

Americans were bombarded with appeals to purchase war bonds. This bond sales booth was set up in lobby of office building at Jackson Boulevard and Franklin Street.

BUY WAR BONDS

Consumers coped with the problems of shortages in different ways. Almost everything was available on the black market, a generic term applied to almost any violation of banned sales, rationing, and fixed-pricing laws. Like the illegal liquor trade during Prohibition, the black market was public enough for consumers to know where banned or rationed items could be purchased, yet usually remained private enough to avoid legal inteference. Some merchants held back nonperishable merchandise from the legal market to be sold for a higher price after its manufacture and sale had been banned. Others accepted secret payments above the fixed price, cheated by substituting inferior merchandise, or dealt in counterfeit or stolen coupons.[47]

Chicagoans found legitimate ways of ameliorating the problems of rationing and controlled prices. Some formed food co-ops as a way to avoid long lines and black market prices at some grocery stores. Others turned to a booming trade in used merchandise, some privately through classified ads. Many charitable organizations opened thrift shops for the first time as fund-raising ventures. Some merely collected a commission for private sales on the premises; others sold donated items. Thousands of Chicagoans followed the suggestion of the OCD newsletter, *Civilian Defense Alert,* and shared gardening tools, sewing machines, vacuum cleaners, and other household goods. This not only helped alleviate shortages, but also created a sense of neighborhood camaraderie.[48]

Selling the War

Shortages, ration coupons, and the need to make substitutions for familiar goods and services left most families with a surplus of cash at precisely the same time that the federal government needed money to fight an expensive war. Economists warned that raising the income tax to fund the war could push the country back into another depression. The Roosevelt administration thus adopted the policy used during World War I: convince Americans to lend surplus income in the form of defense bonds. This would not only divert money away from the black market, but also help restore the sense of economic security that so many people had lost during the 1930s. The biggest challenge was convincing the average citizen to buy a piece of the war.

Federal officials first created measurable goals by staging periodic bond campaigns; by V-J Day, the eighth bond drive was under way. They also made it easy to buy bonds by promoting the volunteer payroll deduction plan, which had been instituted during the late 1930s. Consumers could also purchase ten-cent war-stamps to fill books that were exchanged for an $18.75 bond.

Officials saturated the nation with a sophisticated marketing campaign. Indeed, there were few things as ubitiquous as the reminders to buy bonds. Posters hung everywhere. Neighbors rang doorbells and donated their labor in bond auctions. "Warsages," corsages made of war stamps, became a brief fashion rage. Over twenty thousand Chicago merchants sold them over the counter. At work, companies strove for a Minute Man flag, which recognized that 90 percent of the workers were putting at least 10 percent of their paychecks in bonds. Many corporations and even the state of Illinois invested surplus bank balances in bonds. The campaign to market patriotism was a success.

Bottom, the government used a variety of marketing techniques to finance the war, including eight national war bond campaigns. Below, Chicagoan Harry A. Perlman created these "warsages," which were made of defense stamps.

They also serve, who buy WAR BONDS

7th WAR LOAN

The Kitchen War

Time was the traditional homemaker's master. The 1941 kitchen and what was prepared there differed dramatically from its counterpart of today. Shopping was anything but convenient. There were chain grocery stores, but they were relatively small, and most families continued to buy from independent butcher shops, greengrocers, bakeries, and dairies in the neighborhood. This meant a long walk or trip on the streetcar or in the family automobile. These favorite retailers bought from a system of suppliers who were local, a fact that contributed to the freshness of meat and produce, but it also meant that many fruits and vegetables were available at reasonable prices only during their appropriate seasons. Chicagoans were lucky to be at the nation's rail transportation hub, which assured supplies of Florida and California produce, but high prices often restricted these items to special treats in wintertime.[49]

All food purchases were followed by a race against spoilage. Packaging of dry foods in cardboard or wax paper lacked the ability of today's plastic to preserve freshness and keep out vermin. Because of the depression, many refrigerators were survivors of the 1920s, with notoriously poor freezers. Some families rented small locked cubicles in commercial frozen locker plants, but these were often located an inconvenient distance away. Instead, most consumers relied on canned goods, either their own or store-bought, as a way to halt time between processing and consumption. Thus, with food sources from so many places, and canning as the principal form of food preservation, the Chicago family was highly dependent on a fragile supply line that almost necessitated day-to-day shopping. Those without an automobile faced the additional limit of what they could carry in one trip.

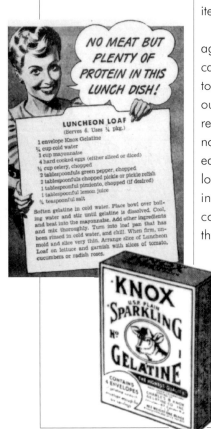

Manufacturers of nonrationed food items were quick to point out how their product could help homemakers stretch their ration points further.

Then came the war. The basis of the food problems that the war generated was a substantially reduced supply that had to be distributed to a more affluent buying public through a transportation system that was already overburdened by wartime demands. The disruption of international shipping all but cut off supplies of many imported items, such as sugar and coffee.[50] Other basic foodstuffs, especially those considered high in protein and energy, were diverted to the military. The army established its largest domestic Quartermaster's Corps operation in a massive warehouse on Pershing Road in the city's central manufacturing district, from which the army coordinated the purchases of mass quantities of food. In 1942, for example, the War Production Board (WPB) took about one-third of all that season's fruit and vegetable pack for the armed forces. Since much of the military consumption was in the battlefield or at sea, government purchasers enjoyed a prior claim on all canned and preserved products.

Civilians had to settle for what was left, but government planners realized that a happy and well-nourished work force was absolutely essential to the successful pursuit of the war. One answer to the food problem was the cultivation of victory gardens, but these produced only a small portion of what was needed. Instead, the supply crisis forced a series of decisions, often unpopular, that modified the free-market supply-and-demand system in an attempt to maintain fair distribution at steady prices. The mechanism was relatively simple at first, but became complicated.

First came a nationwide registration at which every citizen received books of stamps that had to accompany payment when making purchases. Each stamp had to be used during a particular time period. Early in 1944, the government issued supplemental tokens to be used as change—red for the purchase of meat and blue for processed foods. By increasing or reducing the numbers of stamps and tokens needed for each type of purchase, the OPA was able to manipulate consumption away from scarce foods and encourage substitutions with what was plentiful. Government planners, however, soon discovered that the ration system was not enough to keep inflation in check, and the government eventually took control of prices, rents, and wages as well.

Sugar was the first food to be rationed. Between May 4 and 7, 1942, over three million Chicagoans lined up at public schools to fill out the forms to receive a ration book with twenty-eight stamps, each permitting a purchase of one pound of sugar every two weeks. Women who canned their own produce were allowed five extra pounds for their families.[51] Sugar remained in short supply for the duration of the war, forcing changes and substitutes in Chicagoans' diets. Soda pop machines sat empty much of the time, with

bottlers publishing apologetic ads about the difficulties involved in making their product. "The war," grumbled the *Economist*, a local real estate newspaper, "has reached out its monstrous hairy arm into our front yard and snatched the soda pop bottle from our very hands."[52] Although candy production was at an all-time high for military use because it was a quick source of energy, civilians could not find it in stores. The same was true of chewing gum, and midway through the war the William Wrigley Company announced that it was diverting the entire production of its major brands to the military.[53] Restaurants withdrew sugar bowls from tables, dispensing lumps only by request. They found other ways to stretch short supplies: cake frostings got thinner and sweet rolls less sweet, while honey, molasses, and brown sugar found their way into increasing numbers of recipes.[54]

Above, women listen to an OPA representative explain the complexities of rationing. Leather wallets were designed to hold ration coupon books as well as the colored tokens used for change.

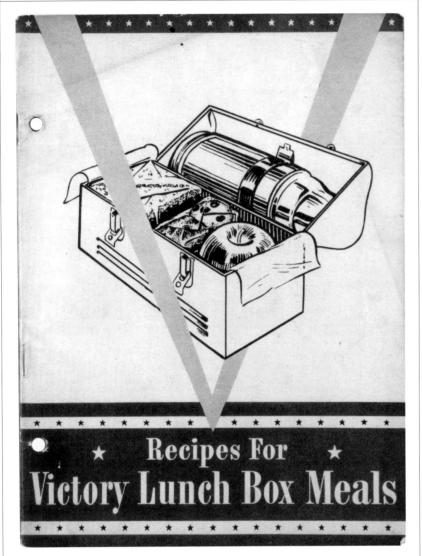

★ Recipes For ★
Victory Lunch Box Meals

The government and food producers encouraged better eating habits for defense workers. They suggested ways to prepare meals without relying on rationed items, such as meat, by substituting eggs, peanut butter, and tinned meats.

Over the next two years the OPA added meats, fats, cheese, butter, coffee, and canned and dried fruits and vegetables to the list of rationed foodstuffs. Throughout the war, Chicagoans faced a series of food problems. Retail prices for canned goods soared, despite government-imposed ceilings on wholesale prices, while rice, canned meats, honey, and dried fruits as much as doubled in price during 1942. Rationing went into effect for canned and dried fruits and vegetables on March 1, 1943, following six days of registration for coupon books.[55] Then, on the following May 17, the OPA imposed retail price ceilings on six hundred varieties of canned fruits and vegetables and a few cuts of meat.

Despite the apparent abundance of livestock in the Midwest, Chicagoans found it increasingly difficult to locate their favorite cuts of meat. At first, the federal government attempted a voluntary rationing approach by launching its "Share the Meat" campaign in October 1942. Civilians were asked to limit their intake of beef and pork to two-and-a-half pounds per week.[56] "Share the Meat" failed, and on March 29, 1943, the OPA instituted meat rationing. For weeks preceding that day, panicky consumers bought everything they could. Crowds gathered hours before butcher shops opened, sometimes standing for hours awaiting the arrival of a wholesaler's truck. Once rationing began, short supplies often prompted consumers to rush out Monday morning and use their entire week's quota of eighteen red tokens on steak, which required the maximum number of points, leaving nothing for late in the week. Others spread their purchases throughout the week, supplementing their menus with fish, poultry, and low-point sausages.[57]

The rationing and price control systems were complicated and frequently confusing. Everyday transactions between consumers and their neighborhood food stores seemed at the mercy of government bureaucracy, as well as the vagaries of the marketplace. The *Daily News*'s complete listing of prices and points covered an entire page with fine print, and all of the city papers ran daily columns or boxes that answered hundreds of questions about unusual situations. For instance, those who purchased home-canned goods from a neighbor technically had to surrender coupons, but no one seemed to know what the sellers were to do with them. Everything was subject to weekly readjustment. On November 22, 1943, for example, the OPA hiked prices on ninety-one foods and lowered them on sixty. Retailers, meanwhile, found themselves swamped with thousands of coupons, which often forced them to hire extra clerks.[58] Despite all the restrictions, prices continued to rise and supplies gradually disappeared. Retailers accused wholesalers, who, in turn, complained about the shippers and the farmers. Everyone blamed the higher wages paid to employees, rapidly increasing transportation and fuel costs, and even skyrocketing costs for seed and animal feed. Government regulators claimed that controls had saved an average Chicago family hundreds of dollars, but many Chicagoans did not believe it.[59]

The Folklore of Shortage

Shortages, rationing, and high prices forced Chicagoans to change their eating habits.[60] Because favorite cuts of meat disappeared, consumers quickly bought out supplies of ocean fish, a commodity made scare by the military disruption of fishing. The major exception was shark, which made its domestic debut during the war. Many tables now held sucker and carp instead of cod and tuna. Homemakers experimented with newspaper recipes for soy beans, which had been virtually unused by consumers since their introduction into the United States in 1907.[61]

The war also reached into the kitchen through the most intense consumer education program in the nation's history. Much of the local activity took place under the guidance of the Chicago Nutrition Committee, which had been founded in May 1942 to help the federal War Food Administration disseminate information about nutrition, recipes, and healthful living. The press and government officials stressed that, as the head of the home economics department of the Illinois Institute of

Technology put it, "the nation is beginning to plan for the first time in its history for a nutrition program."[62]

Wartime propaganda urged homemakers to think of themselves as "home engineers" and thus encouraged them to attend special classes, as well as read and clip the myriad of recipes that appeared in the newspapers. Some turned to *What to Eat, and How to Cook It*, which had been issued by the State Council of Defense during World War I. Others saved the special twenty-two-page *Food For Victory* booklet included in the October 8, 1942, edition of the *Herald-American*. Peoples Gas, which opened its downtown auditorium to frequent classes on saving food, summarized its suggestions in advertisements with headlines such as "Just a Minute Lady," advising smaller helpings, the purchase of seasonable foods only in the quantities needed, and, of course, avoiding unnecessary waste.[63]

As the war progressed, a folklore grew up around the rationing system. At first, some consumers enjoyed the novelty of it. Not long after Pearl Harbor, the *Daily News* instructed readers that the word was pronounced "rayshun." Families tacked rationing guides clipped from the newspapers to the kitchen wall. In the fall of 1943 the *Daily News* described how "ration parties" had become a fad among young married couples. The rules were simple: each couple brought its own food, and sharing dishes was not allowed (which distinguished it from traditional potluck dinners). Commercial establishments of all types, which hoped that consumers would not blame them for the various consumer shortages, gave away special wallets for coupons and tokens. The press reported that West Madison Street transients had found a new source of wine money by selling their books. Rationing even worked its way into the mourn-

ing ritual. On November 17, 1943, Chicago's 560 undertakers announced a new policy: the first interview with the bereaved family would include handing out a preprinted envelope for the return of ration coupons. The OPA presumably read the death notices.[64]

Compromise and Rebellion

The government's rationing and price control system was far from perfect, in part because it forced people to do the opposite of what they had been taught was prudent. Sale prices and impending shortages had always resulted in an urge to "stock up," and when stories began to circulate that rubber goods might become scarce, women rushed to State Street department stores for girdles and corsets. Other rumors caused mass purchases of flashlights, soap flakes, and olive oil. In ordinary times, this panic-buying would have evoked chuckles, but in wartime it became hoarding, which the press condemned as immoral and unpatriotic. "Hoarding Helps Hitler," warned the local civilian defense newspaper. Chicago consumers thus faced the delicate task of balancing patriotism and the desire to preserve some measure of family privacy. Although possession of large supplies of anything did not violate OPA guidelines, lying about what you had on hand to avoid a reduction in the number of ration coupons did. Those caught lying faced a fine and the loss of coupon privileges. For the most part, the OPA relied on veiled threats that they "knew" who had what in their pantries. One grocery store chain used this fear of being apprehended in advertising that it would be happy to buy back excess sugar, which, of course, it resold at a profit.[65]

Shortages also introduced an element of suspicion into the relationship between retailer and consumer. The OPA encouraged citizens to report violations to their block captains, and all across the city and suburbs nervous dealers had to explain to investigators why they ignored rules mandating posted price lists and prohibiting the acceptance of gifts and bribes. Even innocent actions drew suspicion. One dealer claimed that he ground his hamburger in a freezer room to avoid contamination by flies, but the neighborhood OPA price board ordered him to follow regulations and grind it in the presence of customers. There had been too many rumors that butchers were grinding dried animal blood and fat together and calling it hamburger.[66]

Many retailers, in turn, blamed suppliers for encouraging black market conditions, which the Daily News claimed cost Chicago consumers more than $1 million a week in excess charges. Packers and distributors were accused of forcing hidden payments from retailers, along with forcing the purchase of inferior grades and unwanted cuts of meat. Early in 1943 the OPA dispatched more than seventy investigators into Chicago packinghouses, and despite a number of indictments and court-ordered suspensions of business, the problems continued through the rest of the war. Perhaps the most alarming revelation was the entrance of organized crime into the business when former bootlegger Terry Druggan muscled his way into control of a suburban meat supplier. In their defense, packers passed the blame on to ranchers, who in turn, accused feed suppliers.[67]

The food situation became increasingly grim through the closing weeks of 1944 and remained so for the duration of the conflict. By March 1945, market managers were complaining about 25 to 60 percent drops in supplies since winter. Most closed their doors after only an hour or two of business each morning, forcing hundreds of them out of business. Families were left with processed and "stretched" meats such as hot dogs,

sausages, and meatloaf. One such product, Spam, would forever be associated with the war; during some weeks, even that was a luxury. Numerous newspaper stories told of meatless Sundays, where the family gathered around a platter of fried eggs and potatoes as the main course for dinner. What caused the growing crisis? The Tribune blamed it on government policies, claiming that the Roosevelt administration had released enough meat in the weeks before the 1944 election to insure a fourth term, then cut supplies. Incompetent planning accounted for postelection shortages despite record-level farm production.[68]

The OPA blamed the swelling size of the American armed forces for the shortages. In 1941–42, civilian uses claimed 93 percent of processed-food supplies; the military, just 7 percent. During 1944–45, however, the civilian share had fallen to just 59 percent, with the remaining 41 percent going to the military. Sugar inventories also fell to a record low early in 1945, ironically because the fruit crop of the previous year had been large and many people followed the government's suggestion to can all they could grow or buy.[69]

Food shortages tended to undermine the traditional sense of household independence that many Americans thought important. The depression did so by throwing the breadwinner out of em- ployment. Now, with much of the financial independence restored, regulations from Washington determined what a family could buy, not just frivolous items but the basic necessities of clothing and food. Often it became easier, quicker, and even cheaper to turn to outsiders to supply needs that the family had traditionally furnished itself in the home. Commercial laundries prospered, in

"Lady, it's your war, win it!" exhorted one pamphlet on wartime food preparation. Food rationing affected all Americans . Ration stamps (opposite), in addition to money, were required for purchases; change was made with different colored tokens (below), depending on the type of item purchased.

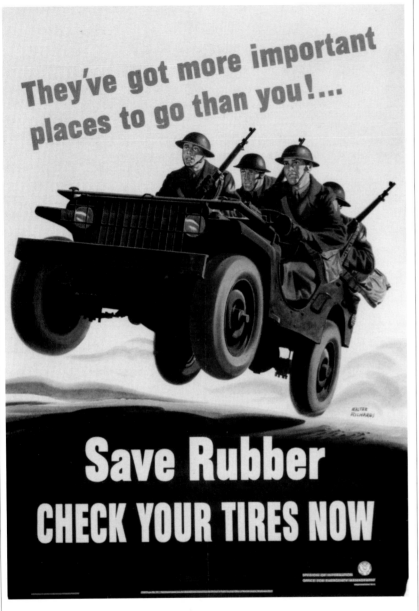

They've got more important places to go than you!...

Save Rubber
CHECK YOUR TIRES NOW

Automobile tires were rationed after America's rubber supply was cut off because of the Pacific war. Because of metal shortages, license plates were manufactured from soybean-based fiberboard.

29 250 ILLINOIS 1944

part because production of home washing machines ceased, and in part because working women did not have time to do the laundry themselves.

Similarly, the shortage of time pushed some traditional food preparation activities outside of the home, especially when both adults worked. Bakery business increased by 45 percent during the first three years of the war. Although families might bake for special occasions, routine breadmaking increasingly disappeared from the home. Commercial bakeshops found that adding vitamins to breads attracted customers, many of whom had to substitute bread and rolls for meat, butter, and cheese. The demand for commercially baked bread proved so great that the Department of Agriculture halted the practice of slicing bread for customers because of the equipment and labor used; the decree was rescinded six weeks later because of public outrage.[70]

Soaring prices and short supplies of foods also undermined the traditional family mealtime. Many Chicagoans preferred to wait for a restaurant table rather than wait for a chicken in a butcher shop. Restaurant food was not rationed to the consumer, although the cook routinely had to make do with less and forced the diner to do the same. Sugar and coffee rationing meant customers got one cup of coffee and one lump of sugar—no refills. Those who ate out also felt cheated by rising prices.

Most restaurants were independently owned, making it more difficult to enforce on them a curb on price increases. During the summer of 1944, the OPA ruled that restaurants had to post their April 1943 menus and prices and charge no more, but this proved almost impossible to enforce.[71]

Getting Around

Chicagoans again faced the dilemma of increased prosperity and dwindling supplies with the restrictions placed on private transportation. Even before the United States entered the war, automobile makers offered "defense" models, which featured painted bumpers and plastic dashboard parts that substituted for chrome and other scarce metals.[72] But Pearl Harbor brought an almost immediate slowdown, then a halt to production, with existing stocks rationed to eager buyers. Used cars soared in value during the early months of 1942, but then, as many younger men waited for the inevitable draft notice, the demand for second-hand vehicles plummeted as well.[73] Dealers, who had finally been experiencing a boom after the decade-long depression, were devastated. Dealerships either closed or began repairing older cars "for the duration."

Tires were even scarcer than cars. The Pacific war cut America off from its once-abundant supplies of natural rubber. Pearl Harbor brought an almost immediate freeze on tire sales until a rationing system could be established. On January 1, 1942, Cook County received the bad news: a new tire quota only 9 percent of normal. The result was a scramble for rubber. Thousands applied for the few hundred rationed tires.[74]

A once-mundane item instantly became precious. Mayor Kelly suggested not only a reduction in driving, but that car owners remove their vehicles from the street to protect tires from the damaging rays of sunlight. A night parking ban, which went into effect in January 1942 to reduce tire theft, was difficult to enforce because only 218,000 of the 650,000 cars registered in Chicago had access to off-street storage.[75] Instead, vulnerable vehicles fed a whole new system of black market sources and sales that developed by early 1942. Tire thieves stripped cars parked on the street and boldly broke into garages. These black market tires sold for as much as fifty dollars each. The tire shortage continued throughout most of the war, but was eased by the rapid rise in synthetic rubber production in 1944–45.[76]

Chicago drivers faced new restrictions when the federal government imposed gasoline rationing to conserve rubber as well as petroleum. If Americans drove less, they would not wear down their tires so quickly. Ample oil supplies staved off this drastic measure in the Midwest, and regional boosters complained that wastefulness on the East Coast, where

This 1942 Hudson was one of the last cars made before wartime production ceased. Even before Pearl Harbor, materials became scarce, and Hudson offered this model with "blackout" features such as nonchrome metal surfaces.

R-556—Rev. 10-1-42

A

MILEAGE RATION

Gasoline was rationed during the war, largely to prevent rubber tires from wearing out. An "A" sticker on a car indicated that the driver was entitled to a gas allocation of three gallons per week.

GAS RATION BOOK

☆

DRIVE UNDER

35

rationing first went into effect, dragged the whole nation into a program that few supported. As was the case with other regulated sales, motorists had a set amount of time to use their gasoline allotments. But unlike the equal rights to purchase other rationed items, gasoline allotments were distributed according to priority needs, which were determined by a neighborhood board. This led to a constant flow of pleas for more gas and complaints about those allegedly cheating. Light driving in one time period led to the temptation to hoard gas for another.

The new restrictions on private auto travel had unexpected consequences. Parking lots stood largely empty.[77] Towing services were overwhelmed with calls from motorists stranded when their old cars broke down or ran out of gas during the last days of an old coupon period. Car owners learned how to fix their own vehicles.[78] City and county police forces put officers back on routine foot pa-

trols, conserving squad cars for emergencies. Despite the inconveniences, rationing and the statewide forty-mile-per-hour speed limit had a positive effect—a dramatic reduction of traffic accidents. Moreover, the gasoline coupon provided police officials with a new way of fining lawbreakers, because local courts approved the confiscation of coupons as a fine for speeding or reckless driving. In mid-1943, violation of citizens' privacy reached the point where the OPA stationed its investigators along major roads to record the license numbers of more than sixteen hundred Chicago vehicles that were far from home during the Independence Day weekend, thus wasting precious gasoline for unnecessary travel. Violators faced a hearing to determine whether their ration books should be canceled.[79]

Most people who could no longer drive helped jam Chicago's privately owned transit systems. After nearly a decade in receivership, their equipment had deteriorated, and there was little money to extend lines to the new outlying defense plants. The widely supported idea of municipal ownership surfaced almost annually through the depression as well as the war, but private bondholders always managed to stop this from happening. Without expanding equipment, the elevated, streetcar, and motor bus companies managed to absorb huge increases in ridership.[80] The city attempted to alleviate the rush-hour problem by encouraging employers to cooperate in a federal program to stagger the hours that workers were required to be on the job; some companies agreed.[81]

The only bright spot in the transit picture was the completion of the State Street subway, which helped untangle Loop traffic. Work began in December 1938 as a depression-era relief project and continued despite the war. It was completed on October 17, 1943.

Shelter and the Changing City

The influx of war workers into Chicago created a severe housing shortage that fed competition for neighborhood space. Housing fell into the same pattern of short supply that plagued every other type of consumer good. Simply stated, there were too many people for too few housing units. The need for new construction was clear, but deciding where and in what ways the building industry could alleviate the situation involved the occasionally indelicate hand of the rationing process.[82]

At the beginning of the war, the housing market was not tight. The relative slowness with which war contracts came to Chicago meant only a limited increase in demand. The housing market turned around dramatically, however, with the influx of workers during 1942. Vacancies plummeted to a record low of 1 percent, while annual rent increases of 10 to 15 percent became common. Tenants complained that landlords demanded outrageous rent increases and hidden payments to insure delivery of a new lease. Occupancy rates, which had been at 95 percent just before Pearl Harbor, reached 98.6 percent in 1942 and an unbelievable 99.7 percent by May 1943.

The shortage meant that few families dared to move. The small amount of turnover came from deaths and the departure of those seeking jobs elsewhere. Those who were forced to move put furnishings in storage until they found a place. The hopeful ones combed the obituaries in search of a potential opening.

City and federal agencies turned to a variety of solutions to the housing crisis. After hearing the pleas, the federal government imposed three basic policies. One was to apply the principle of price ceilings to rented living space. At first, federal housing officials did not think that Chicago warranted rent control, but by March 1942 Mayor Kelly, who

The Chicago Housing Authority gave priority to war workers in their recently completed projects.

had already received fifty thousand complaints from tenants of the city's 600,000 apartments, began to use his influence in favor of a freeze. Landlords were required to register their property with the federal rent administrator and could increase rates only by adding new appliances, which were almost impossible to buy, or by making other substantial improvements and then filling out a petition form.[83] Policies dictated that landlords had to sue to evict a tenant, even when no lease existed. Renters were given veto power over improvements that might increase their rent.[84]

In May 1942 the Chicago City Council attempted to ease the crisis by altering building codes to make it easier to carve houses into apartments and to subdivide larger rental units into small ones. A few months later, the federal government followed with the establishment of the War Housing Center, which not only directed tenants to vacancies, but also served as a clearinghouse for architects, builders, and owners.

Increasing the number of housing units in many neighborhoods meant raising the level of population density, which, in wartime, meant efficiency. The Chicago Plan Commission targeted such areas as Englewood, a South Side community, because it was served by public transit and adjacent to a wide belt of war industries. Conversions were allowed virtually everywhere. Any space with electrical and water and sewer service could get a building permit, including warehouses, stores, lodge halls, and gas stations closed by rationing.[85] The demand for space also prompted building owners to complete a number of the derelict "shells" of buildings that had been left unfinished because of the depression.[86]

Clearly, nothing short of forced billeting of war workers in private homes—a persistent wartime rumor—would allow the existing housing stock to absorb the additional workers expected when the Dodge, Buick, Studebaker, and Douglas plants opened. New construction would have alleviated the problem, but building supplies were scarce. One alternative was the expansion of public housing, which had been a depression-era answer to the twin problems of unemployment in the construction industry and the need to replace slums.

Chicago's first four projects—Jane Addams, Julia Lathrop, Ida B. Wells , and Trumball Park Homes—had been financed but not managed by the federal government.[87] Three days after Pearl Harbor the Chicago Housing

Authority (CHA), established in 1937 to manage the units, broke ground for its Frances Cabrini Homes near Chicago Avenue and Oak Street. And not long after that, work began on the Robert Brooks Homes on the Near West Side. The CHA also modified its rules. Families whose war income exceeded the earlier limits were allowed to stay, while the military, which occupied the Cabrini Homes, and war workers had priority on the long waiting lists for all units built "for the duration."[88] One rule not changed was the racial separation that resulted from a federal policy stipulating that projects mirror the makeup of their neighborhoods. Chicago public housing was therefore overwhelmingly white, with African-Americans allowed only in the Brooks Homes and a small portion of the Addams Homes. Altgeld Gardens, located on the Southeast Side, was set aside for African-Americans working in the Lake Calumet industries. Two new projects, Lawndale Gardens and Bridgeport Homes, were restricted to white workers.[89]

The 10,680 government-financed housing units built in Illinois during the war sharply divided public opinion. When the CHA was ready to fill its new Cabrini project, it received over twelve thousand applications, including two thousand from employers holding defense contracts. Instead, one hundred noncommissioned navy personnel became the first tenants. Applicants appreciated the CHA's attempt to create a genuine sense of community through programs in recreation, child care, health, and tenant self-government. Plans for the seven-thousand-tenant Altgeld Gardens project included its own shopping center.[90]

The private sector deeply resented the wartime expansion of public housing, which had access to land cleared through the use of eminent domain. The Chicago Real Estate Board also complained that the projects were

not assessed real estate taxes, and in the spring of 1943 it launched an unsuccessful effort to change state laws to require collection. The CHA made at least two "voluntary contributions" of $28,190. Private builders also complained loudly that CHA construction costs were excessive and that tenants with incomes as much as three thousand dollars per year were allowed to stay in units costing them fifty-two dollars per month.

At the same time that the inner-city housing market was sustaining the pressures generated by extreme shortages, construction of new industrial complexes and much of the expansion of existing factories happened in the sparsely settled fringe of the city and in the suburbs: Douglas Aircraft in Park Ridge, Buick in Melrose Park, and ALCOA in McCook. The two large plants within the city limits, Studebaker and Dodge–Chicago, stood at the outer fringe of the built-up area. Real estate interests and city planners alike understood the implications of this centrifugal economic pressure on the housing market, especially when commuting conditions were so difficult.

Above, a family in Chrysler Village housing, which was located at Sixty-fifth Street and Long Avenue. Defense workers were given priority in the new public housing projects completed during the war. Opposite above, the Ida B. Wells Homes. Opposite below, Frances Cabrini Homes.

New construction was the obvious answer, but shortages forced what was, in effect, a rationing of building materials. The Federal Housing Authority (FHA) not only decided how many units could be built, but also decreed that housing for defense workers took priority over all other domestic construction. In order to provide more equitable access to materials, it established a six thousand dollar per unit ceiling. The latter posed a special problem in the city, where high land costs left less money for the house. The Kelly administration altered the building codes, despite strong union opposition. New ordinances allowed dry wall construction, basementless slabs or hollow concrete block foundations, shortcuts in the frame design, smaller pipes, and other measures designed to save raw materials. Common-wall row housing was permitted for the first time in decades. When city building commissioner William Schmidt, a distinguished architect, refused to issue construction permits for such buildings, Kelly fired him. The important concession that Kelly did make to skeptical aldermen and worried property-owners, however, was to isolate these "defense homes" in districts separated from existing houses of greater value. Row houses were allowed only where land had been zoned for apartments.[91]

By spring 1942 work was already underway on what would by 1945 amount to nearly twenty thousand units. Economies of scale usually dictated that they be built in clusters of at least ten. Some, like Jeffrey Manor, Damen Park, Princeton Park, and Oriole Park Village, were large subdivisions. Virtually all were built in a wide arc that was at least eight miles from the city center.[92]

The new housing development also spilled into the suburbs, where some of the new industrial plants were successful in applying pressure on the FHA to increase the Chicago

area's housing quota. The opportunity to sell to Douglas workers catalyzed the creation of new subdivisions in Park Ridge, Des Plaines, Schiller Park, and even Franklin Park and Skokie. Dodge–Chicago had a similar effect on the Southwest Side. In addition to "Chrysler Village," a huge apartment complex at Sixty-fifth Street and Long Avenue in the city, builder J. E. Merrion began work on a new town for war workers called Merrionette Park, just outside the city limits. Finally, the ALCOA plant at McCook brought new construction to nearby LaGrange, while the Buick plant resulted in construction of what is presently much of the central area of Melrose Park.[93]

⭐ ⭐ ⭐ ⭐ ⭐ ⭐

In September 1942 the national Office of Civilian Defense (OCD) devised a new goal for patriotic Americans. The award was simple—a red, white, and blue certificate with a large V in the middle—but it symbolized a family's perfect cooperation during trying times. Those who conserved food, clothing, and transportation, collected salvage, took adequate air raid precautions, bought war bonds and stamps, and refused to "spread Axis propaganda" could apply for designation as a "V-home." The following winter, neighborhoods could apply for classification as "V-blocks," and then "V-zones," each step enlarging the scope of perfection.[94]

The list of Chicago's V-homes included those of its first family, Mayor Kelly, on Lake Shore Drive, and James E. Stamps, an African-American living at 6748 South St. Laurence Avenue.[95] The awards to Kelly and Stamps were appropriate, because the requirements for designation mirrored the mayor's vision of a city of near-utopian harmony and cooperation, an idea that seemed to drove local civilian defense efforts. The private homes fit together into neighborhoods, which, in turn, blended seamlessly to make up a great city. The programs that were part of civilian defense, of course, were planned nationally. The names, symbols, and organizational charts came from Washington, but were adapted easily to Chicago neighborhoods. Thus, when a *Daily News* reporter surveyed a sample of V-homes, he found one on a houseboat moored on the North Branch of the Chicago River at Irving Park Road. Another graced the "highest house in Chicago," atop a Loop office building. The old three-flat on the site of Mrs. O'Leary's house on DeKoven Street had one. A Chinatown trading store bore another, as did a house trailer owned by a Sunday School tract salesman.[96]

The irony of it all was obvious. The perfect war family worked long hours overtime, in many cases "loaning" a husband, father, or son to the military and patriotically "made do" with the many disruptions the war brought to their lives. Among the many sacrifices Chicago families made to the defense effort was their basic privacy. Yet, in doing so, they risked their own destruction.

This poster emphasizes the government's message that individuals' efforts on the homefront were vital for winning the war. The service flag and window card were public symbols of individuals' support for the war effort.

Chicagoans rallied in support of the war in many ways. The city sponsored formal plaque dedications honoring Chicagoans killed in the war and their families. Community groups sent food and toiletries, such as the denim bag labeled "Bundles for Bluejackets," to service personnel. Patriotic symbols on everyday items, such as a yarmulke (above) and a decorative pillow (opposite), indicated to others in the community an individual's support for the war effort.

The Neighborhood War

The neighborhood stood halfway between the private world of the home and the events of the larger city. The immediate community had always functioned as the socializer of children and interpreter of national and world events for tens of thousands of newcomers who arrived and took their places in Chicago's history. During World War II, the neighborhood functioned in many ways as it had before. Its schools still educated the young; its shops still fed families; its churches and synagogues still commemorated the milestone events of birth, marriage, and death. Neighbors still gathered to gossip across fences or to chat at streetcar stops or the corner meat market.

But between 1941 and 1945, the functions of the neighborhood expanded. As the war deprived families of food and material goods and the workplace beckoned both men and women, the neighborhood provided what the family could not. More importantly, through the civilian defense effort the neighborhood became the basic building block of the domestic war effort, providing the ideal forum for education and morale-building.

The neighborhood was the mediator, the often-intrusive instructor, and the ever-present collector of money, junk, and anything else needed for the war effort. Civilian defense officers created a citywide network of neighborhood organizations whose attention was focused on carrying out orders from the top, a focus that survived roughly the first two years of the war. During the last half of the conflict, the emphasis shifted to more localized activities.

Chicago was a city of neighborhoods, but it was also a city of ethnic and racial enclaves, making the region a patchwork of attitudes.[1] Some ethnic groups were proud of their close ties to Axis nations; others tried to distance themselves from any association with America's enemies. Unifying these diverse Chicagoans in the common goal of aiding the war effort was one of the biggest challenges civilian defense officials faced.

This Isn't 'Playing Soldier,' This Is War

For more than two years before the United States entered the war, Americans read accounts of the destruction in Europe, learning about how the British survived repeated bombings and organized relief efforts. Now the federal government wanted Americans to believe that it could happen on Main Street, U.S.A., as well.

The fear that Chicago could be attacked by the enemy spurred the Office of Civilian Defense (OCD) to train citizens in a wide variety of skills needed for such an emergency. Opposite, a poster identifying the various insignia used by the OCD.

The responsibility for preparing citizens for enemy attack fell to the civilian defense effort. Civilian defense was structured by a hierarchical chain of command that linked individual households with citywide and national defense networks. One of the civilian defense effort's goals was to sustain interest and morale for the duration of the war, an indeterminate length. Officials tried to do this by simulating wartime conditions of attack and teaching Chicagoans to prepare for it and by keeping alive the fear of subversive activities.

The creation of the civilian defense system was well under way by the time of Pearl Harbor. On May 20, 1941, the Roosevelt administration had established the Office of Civilian Defense (OCD), naming New York's Mayor Fiorello LaGuardia as its director. On August 7, 1941, he designated New York, Chicago, and several other major urban areas as civilian defense districts.[2] Mayor Edward J. Kelly, who assumed the local directorship, had already created the Chicago Commission on National Defense in early March to carry out local tasks such as establishing a servicemen's center, collecting aluminum cans, and creating a register of potential volunteers.

The domain of Chicago's chief executive, one of America's most powerful Democrats, extended across the entire metropolitan area, including the suburbs; this area included half of the state's population. Meanwhile, the national OCD established a civilian defense system on the state government level, and on April 17, 1941, the General Assembly created the Illinois State Council of Defense, later renamed the Illinois War Council.[3] Chicago's role as the hub of Illinois's transportation and communication systems made it a more logical place to coordinate the state's civilian defense efforts than the state capital of Springfield.[4]

There was little in the way of a tangible chain of command for civilian defense until the attack on Pearl Harbor. The immediate response was to assign police to guard duty at bridges out of fear that saboteurs might cripple the city with a few well-placed bombs. On December 21, 1941, in a radio address, Mayor Kelly outlined the building blocks of his plan: six divisions cut into forty districts, two thousand sections, and twenty thousand blocks. Each

level answered to the one above it, with Kelly as coordinator, and Maj. Raymond Kelly, former American Legion Commander, as his chief assistant. The six initial divisions—ultimately increased to seven—coincided with the boundaries of the city's police districts. They shared the same precinct houses, grafting civilian defense to the police department's system of telephone and teletype communications. The hierarchy was soon restructured into 108 communities and then subdivided into zones, then blocks, to conform with the nationwide OCD regulations.

By the end of December, Kelly had begun recruiting volunteers for the block-level jobs. That process took three months, in part because of the time consumed by background checks, and also because Kelly insisted that each block captain be elected by the block residents. This so-called "Chicago Plan" drew national publicity not only for its democratic flavor, but also because it softened the quasi-military character of the whole civilian defense system. On a Sunday afternoon in March at the Chicago Stadium, nearly all of the twenty thousand block captains took their oath of office simultaneously.[5]

In addition to block captain there were thirty-four other neighborhood posts, such as fire warden, victory garden warden, and auxiliary policemen. Civilian defense officials faced a dilemma. Their goal was to involve all Chicagoans in civilian defense efforts, yet the initial volunteer ranks were more than twice the numbers needed. Officials recruited only those most likely to retain their interest in their posts.

The civilian defense hierarchy was standardized across the country, but in Chicago it was superimposed over another citywide organization, the Cook County Democratic party machine, America's last great political machine. Led by Mayor Kelly, Chicago's ma-

chine turned out awesome vote totals for the national Democratic party, and was strengthened through patronage, occasional corruption, and federal depression relief money. The machine and the local war effort were parallel organizations, both designed to unite a diverse and divided city. To a great extent, the war considerably weakened the machine's grip on the electorate. The defense industry boom and the resulting prosperity meant an end to virtually all federal public works projects, thereby eliminating a major source of patronage employment that insured an enthusiastic voter turnout. High-paying factory work also undermined the prestige that a job with the city carried during the depression.[6]

Bernice Narbut Kaufmann
We had teams walking around the block, our square block. . . . We took alternate nights to walk around. We would see if the lights were exposed through the curtains, through the windows, and if they were, we would tell them to pull the shades down. We also gave them hints of what to do in case of an air raid, where to go . . . what to bring with them. . . . As an air raid warden, we had training from the Red Cross . . . But that air raid thing petered out in about six months, so there was not much to do after that.

Most Chicagoans still viewed everything about Mayor Kelly to be politically motivated, even tainted, and that included civilian defense. Even before that organization was in place, Mayor Kelly had to defend his administration against charges that civilian defense would be just another machine-dominated activity. Kelly told a *Daily News* reporter: "When the news of Pearl Harbor reached us, the Democratic organization volunteered for any work it could do. . . . Politics was immediately adjourned and we rallied to our defense without any thought of politics, creed, or color. You can take it from me, there won't be any politics in the doing of this job."[7] The *Daily News* editorialized that "Chicago wouldn't be Chicago if it failed to look for politics in the civilian defense set-up. . . . Chicago will take the mayor at his word and cooperate, it will insist that the word be made good."[8] As the war years passed, there were occasional complaints that precinct captains ran the show, but there is no real way to gauge this charge. When Kelly ran for reelection in 1943, he went "on leave" for four months as the Chicago district's civilian defense coordinator.[9]

As enthusiasm for civilian defense waned during the last half of the war, the political organization assured a sufficient supply of workers to keep the structure functional. And when declining fears of attack prompted the city council to slash the civilian defense budget from $500,000 in 1943 to $250,000 a year later, Democratic party ward organizations made direct cash donations to neighborhood civilian defense groups.[10]

An Experiment in Mass Education

Whatever its motivations, the civilian defense effort appeared initially to be little more than a mass education project. The first stage was to train the trainers; the second, to educate the volunteers. All volunteers took four basic courses prepared in cooperation with the Red Cross: a general introduction, fire fighting, gas protection, and first aid. Those chosen for special tasks went on to appropriate instruction. Although most of the training was concluded by November 1942, the task remained to transform an often-indifferent public into a unified and well-informed group that was ready for war.[11]

The OCD tried two approaches. The first was the medium of electronic communications. Television initially fascinated officials because it disseminated pictures as well as words. W9XBK, the transmitter owned by the Balaban and Katz chain theater operators, was used on December 31, 1942, to broadcast instructional demonstrations to 185 civilian defense headquarters.[12] Radio was more widespread, of course, and thus obviously more useful in reaching the majority of Chicagoans. On March 21, 1942, Albert Lepawsky, a University of Chicago political scientist, began a series of broadcasts on general issues such as intolerance to as many as 300,000 listeners. Three weeks later, the professor abruptly resigned, implying political interference, and OCD officials announced that training would be decentralized into the neighborhoods.[13]

Civilian defense training clearly employed propaganda. Neighborhood Boy Scout troops constantly distributed posters for storefronts, bulletin boards, and utility poles.[14] Civilian defense speakers made hundreds of appearances at meetings of a wide variety of organizations.[15] Taking a cue from museums, city departments erected miniature dioramas depicting the damage a bomb attack might do to municipal facilities and what measures would be taken to restore service.[16] Radio broadcasts reached most homes.

Perhaps the most effective tool, however, was the movie. The central civilian defense command pressed neighborhood headquarters to obtain projectors and supplied long lists of relevant films to show citizens. Some movies, many made in England, demonstrated how to defuse bombs and extinguish phos-

Much of the success of Chicago's civilian defense preparations was due to the participation of individuals on the block and zone level. Civilian defense workers and volunteers learned many skills, such as how to use a gas mask, how to administer first aid, and even how to extinguish incendiary bombs.

Civilan defense gas mask and air raid warden helmet.

phorous fires; others featured moving accounts of British determination, which were regarded as especially inspirational. Late in 1942, *Chicago on Guard* became available. Directed by Noel Smith, best known for his Hollywood action melodramas with canine actors, this twenty-minute film dramatically recreated the city's reaction to Pearl Harbor and underlined the importance of each citizen's contributions. Hundreds of groups viewed it in theaters, basements, garages, and any other place where there was enough space to set up a portable screen.[17]

Chicago's twenty thousand block captains were the cornerstones of the civilian defense effort. They were the major two-way communications conduits. In one direction the message of preparedness flowed from Kelly's office through the neighborhood and to individuals. The official civilian defense telephone, the direct link to central headquarters, was the most essential item in the block captain's office for emergency orders, but most handbills, posters, and other sources of written communication also came through the block headquarters.[18] Many block captains put up a front yard bulletin board, where meeting notices and other information was easily available. Others published newsletters, many of them elaborate monthly publications that indicated substantial donations to the neighborhood OCD treasury, the administration of which was another responsibility of the block captain.[19]

At the same time, block captains gathered information about neighbors and measured the public's mood, reporting such information to civilian defense officials. Because the local block captain asked lifestyle questions that were easily interpreted as an invasion of privacy, he or she had to master the skills of public relations. Early in the war, most people volunteered information about how much sugar or canned goods they had on hand and how many miles they drove each week for ration applications. As the war progressed, they were asked about working hours, number of household members, the interior structure of their home, and whether or not they had an empty room. Most citizens probably never realized that they were not legally required to answer these questions.[20]

The block captains reflected the heterogeneity of the city. They were of all races and nationalities and ranged in age from elderly to as young as eighteen-year-old Sherman Block of North Lawndale. Many were women. "I don't see why other blocks haven't elected women block captains," complained Elizabeth Johnson of Neenah Avenue, who claimed to be the city's first female captain. "It would relieve the men for other duties."[21] Block captains also varied in their enthusiasm and organizational ability. One requirement of the post was to make a map of the block, a task some performed with great zeal, compiling extraordinary amounts of detail about building heights and names of janitors.[22] Others staged elaborate meetings, complete with food, movies, and musical entertainment. In Douglas, a black community on the South Side, for example, Leon Simpson held parades, organized community songfests, set up an outdoor movie projector, and held countless meetings in his headquarters in the Ida B. Wells public housing project. The *Civilian Defense Alert*, however, warned that many block captains used the gatherings for long-winded and self-congratulatory speeches.[23]

Bombing Chicago

While the neighborhood functions of civilian defense instilled a sense of individual participation, a series of blackouts, siren tests, and a mock bombing sought to link home and neighborhood to the citywide preparations for enemy attack. These exercises had several practical uses. They tested the effectiveness of individual block leaders, allowing officials to determine who was really effective. They also helped to smoke out or at least embarrass slackers by demonstrating that a vast majority of their neighbors were cooperating. These drills also graphically demonstrated to each citizen how they, their block, their zone, and their neighborhood fit into a larger network. These well-publicized events boosted enthusiasm. David Slight of the University of Chicago told a City Club forum that "blackouts cannot build morale, for morale is built by character and responsibility. But blackouts can build understanding of the issues we face. . . . I personally think that one of the finest things that could happen in Chicago would be a blackout."[24]

Preparations for Chicago's first blackout proceeded through stages from citywide public spaces down to the individual home. Planners first tried to determine the most efficient way to shut off the maximum number of lights. City streetlights were no problem, and many large corporations cooperated by shutting off their huge signs "for the duration." But it took a new ordinance, surveys, an elaborate pamphlet, and visits by block captains to darken the tens of thousands of commercial advertising signs. The city finally demanded that store owners install an exterior switch that would shut off all lights, including those left burning to thwart burglars.[25]

City officials made it clear that the safest place for Chicagoans to be during a bomb attack was in their homes. Oscar Hewitt, pub-

WHAT TO DO IN AN AIR RAID

CHICAGO METROPOLITAN AREA

OFFICIAL BULLETIN

OFFICE OF CIVILIAN DEFENSE, CHICAGO METROPOLITAN AREA
EDWARD J. KELLY, UNITED STATES COORDINATOR

August, 1942

Early in the war, the fear of an enemy air raid attack on Chicago was very real. Air raids were to be expected here, cautioned this OCD pamphlet, pointing out that Axis aircraft could conceivably attack Chicago by flying over the North Pole from occupied Norway.

lic works commissioner, noted that only 31 percent of Chicago's 212.86 square miles was occupied by residential dwellings and their surrounding lots. This meant that, statistically at least, Chicagoans who retreated behind their own doors had less than a one in three chance of being hit by random bombing.[26] It also meant that OCD officials' biggest job was preparing Chicagoans for the possibility of explosive and incendiary devices falling from the sky into their homes and yards. Neighborhood store window displays showed families what was needed to prepare for enemy attack: buckets, sand, a metal garbage pail, shovels, a portable radio, candles, and blankets.[27]

Inventors and entrepreneurs quickly improved on the design of basic necessities or repackaged existing products to capitalize on the defense boom. There were several types of fire extinguishers to douse phosphorous bombs and put out other fires. Window shade

Susan Waldman
Do you remember the air raid, the big air raid to put the civilian defense into action? Boy am I glad we weren't attacked! Different bombs had different crepe paper streamers. Red I know were incendiary bombs. . . . And whatever kind of bomb it was, it was supposed to be treated according to instructions. Incendiaries were supposed to be sprayed with a fine mist of water, otherwise they would go up. And I think there was a green one; if a green one fell on you, forget it, you're out! Well, our air raid wardens were so well trained. They just went around picked them up, threw them in a bucket! And I remember thinking to myself, "that's wrong, you're not supposed to do that!"

manufacturers introduced several types of blackout curtains and an adhesive material that could be put on the windows in a hurry. Folding door manufacturers produced the light-proof "Folding Fabric Blackout Partition." Fireproof paints, speedy sandbag fillers, shatterproof boards for windows—the many new civilian defense products led Chicago's Dartnell Corporation, a business publisher, to introduce a magazine called *Civilian Defense*, which described innovations and published test results of the products.[28]

The most difficult obstacle officials faced in linking the home through the neighborhood to the citywide defense network was establishing an effective air raid alarm system. A special air raid siren test on April 15, 1942, was unheard in many neighborhoods. The city then appropriated $150,000 for forty-three new steam and electric sirens, which were jointly developed by Bell Laboratories and the Chrysler Corporation. On October 28 a test of 508 public and private sirens finally reached the entire city.[29]

By the spring of 1942, Chicagoans were wondering whether there would ever be a citywide blackout of the type that had already become common on the East and West coasts. On July 8, 1942, the city council passed a special blackout ordinance that endowed civilian defense workers with municipal police powers and enumerated a number of acts that became illegal during both practice and actual blackouts and air raids: loitering, remaining in groups of more than four, allowing lights to shine, and doing anything else that might be considered obstructive.

On the night of August 12, 1942, Chicago, in the words of one observer, "lay in deep slumber as though a huge handkerchief, saturated in chloroform, had been pressed against its face."[30] About fifteen minutes of darkness—judged 95 percent effective—followed, as the news media and city officials looked down from tall buildings and airplanes.

The press played up certain acts of compliance, such as priests at Holy Family Church blowing out altar lights that had burned continuously since the church survived the Great Fire of 1871. The 21,422 ground observers were more interested in such overlooked light sources as smokers' lit cigarettes, glowing radio tubes, and lamps left near leaky window coverings.[31]

Two months later, on October 7, Chicago participated in a second type of blackout, which city officials claimed to have invented. This "camouflage light test" followed the standard blackout procedure, except that travel was allowed on side streets. This philosophy of defense assumed that enemy bombers would be confused by the unusual light pattern and be diverted away from strategic targets. Compliance with this test, which was held at 2:45 A.M., was voluntary; most Chicagoans slept through it.[32]

By the middle of 1943, it was difficult to sustain the belief that Chicago was vulnerable to enemy attack. As public interest began to

wane, local OCD officials decided to stage their most spectacular exercise, a mock bombing that took place on May 23, 1943. On that dark and rainy Sunday afternoon, more than one hundred planes from the Illinois Civil Air Patrol dropped 210,000 newspaper wads, each with a color streamer that indicated the type of bomb it was supposed to represent: red for incendiary, blue for high-explosive, yellow for gas, and green for unexploded or delayed-action. Citizens were instructed to let civilian defense personnel pick up the "bombs," and most people complied. Officials were generally pleased with the results, although only 42 percent of the "bombs" were recovered. "This is thrilling," Mayor Kelly told a reporter, "It shows Chicago is prepared."[33]

The Enemy Within

By the time the mock bombing took place, the fear of enemy attack had largely disappeared from the minds of Chicagoans. The real fear was that of sabotage, and the average citizen could do nothing about that except remain alert. Occasional spy and sedition cases gave some credence to this fear. Through most of the war there were references to the Bund, a pro-Nazi organization. On June 23, 1942, Chicago police padlocked Haus Vaterland, the Bund's headquarters at 3857 North Western Avenue.[34]

The most spectacular espionage incident, however, began during the summer of 1942 with the arrest of German spies, one of whom was twenty-two-year-old Herbert Haupt. Naturalized as a child, Haupt had grown up in Chicago, where his parents still lived. He had been trained in a Nazi spy school in Germany and had returned to Chicago to bomb war plants. Arrested on June 27, 1942, he was soon tried and convicted, and on August 8 he was executed. Haupt's parents, Hans and Erna

Haupt, as well as an aunt and uncle and the parents of a friend, were arrested for harboring a spy and assisting in espionage. They were tried and sentenced to life imprisonment. After the war, they were deported.[35]

While the Haupt case seized international headlines, it was an isolated incident. Nonetheless, the *Civilian Defense Alert* claimed that there was an increase in enemy activity in January 1943 and instructed its readers how to reach federal authorities to report suspicious activities. It reassured citizens that the Radio Intelligence Division of the Federal Communications Commission monitored, recorded, and investigated all suspicious radio transmissions within fifty miles of the city. By the end of the year, the OCD had reportedly sworn in a number of milkmen to listen to the conversations of suspicious families.

It was also difficult to sustain even fear of the threat of any

Left, this powerful British poster, which was distributed in the United States, stresses the danger of internal sabotage. Below, this small slip of paper reveals the distrust some Americans had for citizens of German ancestry. It was found in the papers of a West Lake View OCD precinct commander who spoke with a pronounced German accent. Opposite, authorities at the local OCD headquarters plan a mock bombing of Chicago.

Get the hell out of town, you Nazi — or we drive you out.
The True Americans

Above, members of the Back of the Yards community erect an honor roll of residents in military service. Below right, members of the West Lake View civilian defense district display the results from a food drive to benefit local servicemen's centers.

massive plot of internal alien subversives rooted in local ethnic communities. Few people during World War II doubted the loyalty of Chicago's German-Americans. The Haupt case, as the local ethnic leadership eagerly pointed out, was a rare exception. But German-Americans wanted to avoid even a hint of disloyalty. They canceled plans for a mass loyalty meeting early in 1942 for fear of even suggesting nationalist sentiment. The *Civilian Defense Alert* did its part by carrying positive stories, such as a fictional piece about an old German immigrant whom neighbors suspect of disloyalty because of his absence at neighborhood activities. The happy ending comes with the discovery that he wanted to help, but his poor hearing made him unaware that the block captain was at the door.[36]

Not even fears of spies and saboteurs, however, could sustain interest in the civilian defense effort in its original form. Instead, the local block organizations moved on to new activities. As a *Tribune* year-end summary for 1943 put it, "No longer was the OCD prepared to battle the intangible terrors of theoretical invasions. Its efforts were changed, designed to shorten the war." In effect, the activities that Mayor Kelly had initially promoted as a way of softening the militaristic image of central command now became the main concern of the block captains and their crews.[37]

The Importance of Community

As the fear of enemy attack subsided, Kelly became increasingly aware of the contradictory nature of civilian defense itself: on one hand, he needed a centralized command structure; on the other hand, he wanted to avoid the appearance of a morale-eroding dictatorial structure. One solution was to transform civilian defense into a multifaceted service organization. As the months passed, Kelly's central OCD office began to pass more responsibilities on to the neighborhood level. When housing grew scarce because of the influx of defense plant workers, block captains were called upon to survey the houses under their jurisdictions for vacancies.[38] In June 1942 Kelly launched a crusade against noxious weeds, which caused a high worker absenteeism rate among the 150,000 Chicagoans who suffered from hay fever. When the city council passed a law calling for fines for those who allowed such weeds to grow on their property, the block captains surveyed the problem and issued warning notices.[39] They also collected binoculars for the navy, helped consumers understand rationing and price control guidelines, provided information about the draft, distributed emergency fire sand buckets, and distributed the *Civilian Defense Alert*. Civilian defense groups also became essential to the war bond drives.[40]

Kelly spoke of civilian defense as an important tool in building a utopian sense of community. In April 1942, the *Civilian Defense Alert* announced that "decentralization is at hand. The OCD, Chicago Metropolitan Area, can now progress only if community commanders take over the reins and drive from here on."[41] The mayor insisted that the role of the central office should be merely that of initiator. Block-level democracy installed the best leaders, who were responsible for bringing the block together in a neighborly spirit that revived the traditional town hall meeting. Communities held rummage sales and "get acquainted" parties. Neighbors looked out for each other's safety as well. In three well-publicized incidents, OCD lookouts rescued several people from a large apartment house fire in Kenwood, found a kidnapped child on the West Side, and chased a home invader out of the Humboldt Park area.[42]

Kelly's thrust toward decentralization coincided with the growing importance of the neighborhood as a basic unit of other home-front activities. The draft board was one obvious example. There were 151 local draft boards in Chicago, as well as an advisory board for registrants in each of the city's fifty wards; suburban Cook County had twenty-nine boards, DuPage, four, and Lake, three. State selective service officials took great care to balance the ethnic and racial makeup of each board to match that of the community.[43] The OPA also established local boards to review complaints and monitor adherence to rationing and price controls. When point rationing arrived, local civilian defense organizations took over the function of consumer education. The Central Uptown group, for example, set up a model store at 1063 West Argyle Street to educate the community's sixty thousand residents.[44]

Neighborhoods also assumed a growing role in providing wholesome and patriotic activities for youngsters, in part as a substitute for working parents. The variety of activities was endless. Children were essential to the scrap drives, and several neighborhoods staged elaborate parades to celebrate "Uncle Sam's Scrappers."[45] In the Marquette Park area, the thirty-five-member "Freedom Flute Band" played at over forty gatherings. Kids near Broadway and Pensacola avenues on the North Side volunteered their wagons as substitutes for motorized grocery and hardware store deliveries. Others washed cars and performed household work to raise funds for defense activities.[46]

Some neighborhood youth activities were sponsored by branches of larger organizations. The Boy Scouts, Girls Scouts, and Camp Fire Girls all performed heroic amounts of public service.[47] The American Youth Reserves, headed locally by Kenneth "Tug" Wilson, well-known athletic director at Northwestern University, combined patriotic instruction, community service, and physical education for youngsters between the ages of eight and nineteen. Underlying its service activities was the goal of instilling discipline and combatting delinquency.[48]

Boy Scouts and other youth groups enthusiastically participated in scrap drives and other neighborhood activities.

Finally, the neighborhood softened the private pain of separation left in the wake of a loved one's departure into the military service. When the last goodbyes were said at the curb or the train station and the small flag with the blue service star went up in the living room window, neighbors looked to each other for support. The neighborhood played an increasingly supportive role as the war progressed. At first, each block erected an honor roll listing the names of young men and women who had gone to war. Crude at first—usually a simple painted board attached to a flagpole—these not only became more elaborately decorated as the months and years passed, but the dedication of the honor rolls became standardized as an activity of the local civilian defense organization. Speeches and patriotic music were part of the formulaic dedications.[49]

As the war progressed and more and more young Chicagoans died in action, the neighborhood also assumed the duty of mourning with its families. Families who lost a loved one put a gold star decal in their window. In the summer of 1943, the city civilian defense organization announced a plan to honor fallen soldiers by erecting a memorial plaque and naming a neighborhood intersection, officially designated a square, after him or her. All over the city, Chicagoans who lost relatives to war joined in the solemn unveiling ceremonies.[50]

Right, neighbors in the Back of the Yards watch the unveiling of an honor roll listing residents in service. Below, the Gold Star Mothers Club of Chicago Heights poses with their flags. Each star represents a son or daughter who died in the war.

Fighting the Axis with Rake and Hoe

The expanding spectrum of neighborhood functions depended in large part on the enthusiastic support generated by such shared activities as victory gardening. Here private family self-interest and public patriotism fused. Interest in this activity predated Pearl Harbor. During the defense build-up, many agricultural laborers had departed for better jobs, resulting in spot shortages of some produce items. As the overburdened national transportation system began to bog down by the winter of 1941–42, government planners lowered the priority of long-distance produce shipments. It then became logical to localize food-growing as much as possible. As George Donoghue, head of local OCD victory garden activities put it, "Cartridges have priority over carrots in boxcar space. Thus, you ease the burden on the railroads and truck lines when you grow those carrots yourself. You also free the hand of the undermanned farmer for fuller war production."[51]

Amateur gardening was not new to Chicago. During the last decades of the nineteenth century, settlement house and charity workers had encouraged the poor to cultivate vacant plots in congested slum neighborhoods. Vegetable cultivation occupied idle time, gave a sense of self-worth, and provided a measure of self-sustenance that reduced dependence on welfare. During war, however, "vacant-lot gardening" became "victory gardening," and its most enthusiastic supporters were consumers who wanted to avoid standing in line at the produce stand.[52]

While a somewhat loosely organized program had been successful during World War I, the new war brought a remarkable level of organization, in which this casual activity was subsumed into the patriotic hierarchy. In January 1942 the national OCD urged local officials to take over the direction of the activities. Mayor Kelly soon proclaimed victory gardening a part of his defense operation and appointed a gardening officer for each of the 108 civilian defense communities. Within two months, officials had obtained the use of tractors for plowing, set up criteria for approving plot sites, established a schedule of community meetings and lectures, and published a how-to pamphlet.[53]

Victory gardening succeeded for several reasons. The crusade adapted itself to the variety of neighborhoods and lifestyles in the region. The OCD issued suggestions about what crops should be planted where, based primarily on the amount of space available and the amount of sulphur in the air. The OCD pamphlet suggested underground root crops, such as carrots, turnips, and beets, for congested industrial districts. In addition to these, vegetables such as tomatoes, peppers, and cabbage were suitable for outlying residential areas where the air was cleaner. Gardens in the semirural parts of the region, where plots could be large, were ideal for eggplant, sweet corn, and vining plants, such as cucumber and squash.[54]

Victory gardening also attracted widespread attention from private interests whose own goals became identical with the patriotic good. Civic organizations such as the Kiwanis recruited gardeners, while employers encouraged the formation of "victory garden clubs" as a productive idle-time activity for their workers.[55] The newspapers devoted their Sunday gardening columns to the cause, while the *Herald-American* provided window decals for participants. The Fair, a Loop department store, opened an extensive gardening section and sponsored the "Gardening Fair of the Air," a daily radio program on WIND.[56] Gardening clubs, some of

Chicagoans were encouraged to plant victory gardens to ensure there was enough food for everyone.

Victory gardeners cultivated vacant land even in densely populated parts of the city. Several organizations, including the Chicago Park District and the OCD, offered instruction on how to grow successful urban gardens.

which had fallen into inactivity during the depression, conducted classes and contests. Grocers realized that rather than producing competition, the home-gardening crusade actually increased business by introducing customers to new vegetables, such as Swiss chard and kohlrabi.[57]

Like bond drives and other homefront activities, the gardening crusade developed goals for participants. Neighborhood OCD officials awarded ribbons and war bonds for excellence, while the newspapers published lists of superachievers. The *Chicago Sun* held its first citywide Harvest Festival at Soldier Field in September 1943. Amidst displays and demonstration plots, thousands of amateur gardeners showed off their best produce and collected awards.[58]

Most importantly, perhaps, victory gardening helped create a sense of community by breaking down the barriers of anonymity that characterized city life.[59] These activities varied according to the density of the neighborhood. As the *Civilian Defense Alert* put it, "Victory gardens are to the outlying communities and divisions what flag poles are to the more densely populated sections."[60] In several cases, neighbors set up roadside stands to sell excess production, donating the proceeds to the local OCD.[61] Meanwhile, the Chicago Housing Authority established gardens to help generate neighborliness in its new projects.[62]

As with other homefront activities, interest in victory gardening suffered a sharp decline in 1944. By the end of March, seed sales had begun to decline, as did attendance at gardening lectures. Experts credited a surplus of canned vegetables from 1943, as well as the removal of point rationing from many commercially canned vegetables. False optimism about an early end to the war no doubt contributed, as did the lethargy that was the inevitable result of two years of sustained enthusiasm. Those who left their ground fallow, however, later regretted it, as the food shortages of late 1944 and early 1945 left some tables bare, and military setbacks that year made it seem that the war was not going to end soon. Victory garden officials reported, however, that 1945 brought renewed interest.[63]

Get in the Scrap

The nationwide scrap drives also linked the war, the neighborhood, and the private household. They elevated individual effort to a place of importance in the community patriotism. Before Pearl Harbor, increased aircraft production had already prompted a nationwide effort to collect aluminum, but it had been a haphazard campaign. Housewives willingly donated their aluminum cookware and anything else of substance to the drive, but no one in December 1941 could have guessed how important these donations would eventually be to the war. The campaign, in the words of the Daily News, was "just beginning to scour Chicago for scrap."[64]

While the government exhorted Americans to save metals, rubber, and a few types of paper, officials directed their initial efforts at large potential sources of scrap, such as railroads, manufacturers, retailers, and large corporations. The Chicago and North Western Railroad revealed that it had scrapped 236 locomotives since 1939.[65] Similarly, Chicago's five hundred shoe repair shops promised to collect worn rubber heels and nails, while Sears instituted a policy of buying back golf balls for the salvageable rubber.[66]

Corporations were the first targets of the drive to conserve paper use and increase collections of waste paper. The State Council of Defense sold the idea through its own advertising campaign. "You're a Soldier in This War," advised a brochure sent to office managers asking them not to waste paper clips, stationery, pencils, and other supplies. They were asked to scour their buildings for waste paper, rags, scrap metals, and old rubber. The Walgreen Company, Service Drugs, National Tea Company, S. S. Kresge, F. W. Woolworth Company, and Kroger Grocery and Baking Company were among those that promised to cooperate. In return, they were

allowed to display a colorful "Salvage for Victory" decal.[67] The Chicago Association of Commerce asked businesses to eliminate unnecessary paperwork, reduce the size of forms, and reuse interoffice envelopes. It urged factories and offices to institute a separate collection box for each type of paper and bale what they gathered.[68]

Not even the most thorough housecleaning by businesses, however, could produce enough scrap, and officials next targeted residential neighborhoods. Here, three types of citizens, each with a special knowledge of where to find salvageable material, were enlisted. Janitors, who controlled the flow of discarded material from buildings located in densely settled neighborhoods, were asked to stop burning paper and to pick through everything discarded by tenants.[69] In outlying neighborhoods, where families were larger and most people lived in single-family dwellings,

Pamphlets reminded Chicagoans how valuable scrap was to the war effort.

salvage officials targeted children. The youngsters, whose knowledge of vacant lots and alleys was often more intimate than that of adults, incorporated collecting in their play, staging parades, house hunts, and parties.[70]

Finally, the backbone of the conservation effort was Chicago's homemakers. The paper salvage campaign preached what the depression had already taught: the need for substitution and economy. Enthusiastic newspaper articles reminded homemakers to take their own baskets to the market, thereby eliminating the need for paper bags, to save egg cartons and cleaners' bags for reuse, to dry and incinerate garbage, and to use oil cloth instead of paper, saving the newspapers instead for collection. Neighbors were asked to pool their bales so that the city's three thousand scrap and junk dealers could collect it more efficiently.[71]

The best-organized scrap drive aimed at homemakers was the search for fat. "WOMEN OF CHICAGO . . . WILL YOU HELP TO AVENGE PEARL HARBOR AND WIN THE WAR," commanded one advertisement, "SAVE ALL COOKING FATS AND GREASES USUALLY WASTED! YOUR COUNTRY NEEDS THEM."[72] Mayor Kelly claimed credit for this campaign. Several months before Pearl Harbor, one of Kelly's advisors had read that every one hundred pounds of reclaimed fat would produce sixty-one pounds of dynamite. Japanese military action in the Pacific had cut off one major source of fats, but about two-thirds of that amount could be replaced by the estimated one billion pounds discarded each year in American homes.[73]

Organized scrap drives proved remarkably successful. Right, children were especially helpful in gathering materials that could be converted into defense goods. Below, this huge pile of aluminum scrap was collected at Michigan Avenue and Congress Parkway in July 1941 during Aluminum Roundup Week.

In the early months of 1942, the entire nation adopted Kelly's plan. Red-white-and-blue receptacles for donations adorned many street corners, but most homemakers earned extra money by selling the fat back to the neighborhood butcher, receiving four cents a pound for dark fats, a nickel for the more desirable white. Retailers, in turn, were paid a penny a pound for their cooperation when they turned the fat over to the government.[74] Newspaper columns, advertising, and brochures distributed by block captains answered questions such as what to do with bones, how to separate out juices, and why it was critical to save even the smallest dab of fat.

By June 1942 the nationally organized drive for rubber and tin was focused on the home and neighborhood. Nathaniel Leverone, Illinois's War Production Board salvage director, accurately predicted in June 1942 that "Chicagoans will be subjected to one of the most intensive campaigns ever conducted to salvage every available scrap of rubber from girdles to garden hoses stored in closets, basements, alleys, offices and factories." Any type of scrap rubber could be reprocessed. Leverone offered two inducements to citizens: the payment of a penny a pound for rubber turned in to service stations, and the possibility that an ample rubber supply might help Illinois avoid gasoline rationing, which was intended to save rubber by reducing mileage.[75]

The hunt was on. Volunteers scoured vacant lots and junk yards, which were dubbed "rubber mines." Teams organized by Scout troops and block captains competed for prizes. Old swim caps, dolls, ice cube trays, hot water bottles, eye droppers, bath mats, and even fountain pen bladders were highly coveted. One candy company donated 2.1 million rubber toys marked "Made in Japan."[76]

Homemakers saved waste cooking fats and sold them to their butchers for a few cents per pound. Fats were converted into glycerine for explosives.

Sandee Grossman
You know when you [recycle] you sort of feel like you're doing something? Well that's the feeling we had all the time! The recycling is bringing back memories to me of participating and helping my country. And we had that feeling all the time.

Volunteers around the city mobilized for the scrap collection efforts.

The tin campaign got off to a somewhat rockier start. Through the spring of 1942 government officials had told Chicagoans not to bother saving tin cans because there were no local detinning plants that were capable of reclaiming the 1 to 3 percent of tin from each can. On June 15, 1942, however, the "save-your-can" crusade began. Consumers were asked to peel off labels, remove both ends, and flatten the can for neighborhood collection. Communities competed for prizes; Kenilworth won with a total of 5,850 pounds by the end of 1942.[77]

The metal scrap drives of late 1942 took on a sense of desperation, highlighted by acts of publicity-generating showmanship and symbolic acts. The Chicago Historical Society donated slave chains, and the Great Lakes Naval Training Center gave fifty cannonballs and a gun the from USS *Maine* to the effort.[78] Businesses and homeowners checked their roofs for old radio antennas, which contained copper. Companies honored employees for metal-saving ideas and heroic collection efforts.[79] When the results of the drive were tallied, Chicago led the nation with an average of 113.7 pounds of scrap per capita.[80]

The conclusion of the 1942 campaign marked a peak in the public's enthusiasm for the scrap drives. What had been novel, patriotic fun, however, became a boring routine. To some extent, the city had also been picked clean of some types of salvageables. Early the next year the Illinois War Council privately admitted that it was battling rumors that the national quota had been filled for the remainder of the war. A new copper and brass campaign called for the "complete mobilization" of Chicago's 650,000 children, the group whose interest seemed the most durable.[81]

Meanwhile, the fat campaign encountered an unexpected problem. Meat shortages meant that the average household produced less rendered fat. Despite renewed sloganizing that urged Chicagoans to "keep the frying pans pouring dynamite to keep the guns loaded," the OPA resorted to rewarding cooperation with extra red ration points, so that consumers could buy more meat. Even so, by March 1944 the Illinois War Council warned that the rationing of soap, which was manufactured with fat, might be necessary.[82] Similarly, Chicago's tin can collections for the first six months of 1944 were 60 percent below that of the previous year, despite urgent pleas that tin was needed for solder for vital electrical equipment.[83]

The only really successful campaign for the remainder of the war was a renewed paper salvage drive that included brown paper, cardboard, and anything else that might be converted to packing cartons. "Our Wastebasket Goes to War," headlined a *Daily News* cartoon, which explained that it took five pounds of wastepaper to make a single waterproof supply carton for the armed forces.[84] By the time it was over at the end of August 1944, Chicagoans had collected over five thousand tons of paper, a whopping 38 percent of the national total.[85]

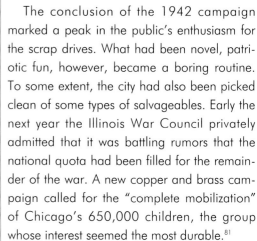

WASTE PAPER
CURB COLLECTION
SATURDAY April 28TH
This paper Donated By Hotel Sherman

Many Chicagos

Chicago's city hall also dominated salvage drives and other civilian defense activities in the suburbs. Mayor Kelly's jurisdiction reached north to Waukegan, west to Wheaton and Naperville, southwest to Lemont, south to Chicago Heights and into North, Hobart, and Calumet townships in Lake County, Indiana. Within it lay a variety of lifestyles and approaches to the national emergency.[86] Evanston drew upon the knowledge of Northwestern University professors and involved five thousand residents directly in specialized classes.[87]

Less densely settled suburban districts made their own adjustments. Every one of the five hundred blocks that made up Berwyn, for instance, had a "Know Thy Neighbor" club that met in a home rather than in a public building. While the Berwyn groups conducted all of the usual classes and drills, the emphasis was clearly on creating tight-knit social groups.[88] The open spaces of Lombard allowed yet another variation. As the *Daily News* put it, "civilian defense is interpreted by a group of sportsmen to mean the training of as many persons as possible in the safe and proper use of firearms to defend their homes against domestic lawlessness or foreign enemies."[89] In sparsely settled farming districts such as Arlington Heights, many volunteers had to combine offices and keep in contact with dispersed membership on farms.[90]

Civilian defense adapted its programs to differences in the physical locations and population densities of neighborhoods. Even before Pearl Harbor, the Slavic and Mexican neighborhoods adjacent to the steel mills of the Southeast Side felt vulnerable to enemy attack. Approximately 75 percent of their workers were directly engaged in defense production, and the area was the site of four giant steel plants, two grain elevators, a pair of electric

Chicagoans enthusiastically raised funds to finance military equipment. It took only forty days to collect money for the heavy cruiser USS *Chicago*, pictured above at its christening. The ship replaced the first *Chicago*, which was sunk in January 1943. Left, the women of B'nai B'rith conclude a successful fund-raising drive to purchase navy airplanes.

generating plants, six railroads, and a chemical company. Informal defense classes had already begun in March 1941, and December 7 brought almost universal participation for residents.[91] By contrast, Hyde Park residents, usually described as aloof apartment dwellers, participated far less enthusiastically.[92]

Block organizations also mirrored Chicago's patchwork of nationalities, although the city of December 7, 1941, was somewhat less ethnic than it was during World War I. The continuing cutoff of immigration had made it difficult for many of the thousands of

Many Chinese-Americans, fearful that they would be mistaken for Japanese, wore buttons to proclaim their heritage and their patriotism.

ethnic organizations to replace older members who had died. The Great Depression had also seriously hurt some ethnic organizations, especially benevolent and savings and loans societies. Hard times forced many to eke out a means of survival. The Americanization process advanced more quickly among the young. But ethnicity survived in the form of churches and synagogues, social and benevolent organizations, newspapers and radio stations, and small businesses. And during the war, one of every five Chicagoans was foreign-born.

Chicago's ethnic neighborhoods held widely differing opinions about the alliances Americans made to fight the war, especially the United States' link with the Soviet Union. The American-Russian alliance made Russian friendship suddenly popular. The local Russian War Relief Society held clothing drives, which were warmly supported across the city. Russian culture became fashionable. The local press reviewed Soviet movies, and even the *Civilian Defense Alert* turned music critic, explaining to its readers that Dmitri Shostakovich's Seventh Symphony, written during the Siege of Leningrad, "now emphasizes rather than diminishes his renown as the Soviet Union's outstanding fire warden."[93]

But not everyone was charitable toward the Soviet Union. In 1944 some of Chicago's Greek-American leaders blamed Joseph Stalin for the civil war in Greece and warned about Soviet efforts to establish dictatorships in their homeland.[94] The Polish community was also divided over the American alliance with the Soviets, with heads of various Polish-American organizations cheering when the Russians moved across the prewar Polish border in January, but others warning later in 1944 that Stalin was not to be trusted.[95]

Ethnic neighborhoods found many avenues through which to express their patriotic sup-

port for the American war effort. Groups such as the "Comité Contra El Eje," or Anti-Axis Committee, promoted patriotism in the city's Mexican-American community.[96] The return of prosperity had refilled the depression-depleted coffers of organizations, and many groups, such as the Lithuanian Roman Catholic Alliance, Polish National Alliance, Italian Sewer and Tunnel Workers Union, and the Croatian Fraternal Union of America, purchased defense bonds. The Chinese community purchased prodigious amounts of war bonds, raising funds with events such as a Chinatown parade led by a 150-foot dragon. And, in one show of patriotism held shortly before Italy left the war, ten thousand of Chicago's Italian-Americans bought more than one million dollars worth of bonds in a single afternoon.[97]

Homefront activities also brought Chicago's ethnic women from their homes. Along with their native-born counterparts, they were the cornerstone of the neighborhood Red Cross, which organized local branches along nationality lines. There were groups affiliated with hundreds of sewing societies, educational alliances, woman's clubs, churches, and synagogues. Members made bandages, took nursing classes, collected money, and operated blood drives.[98]

For many ethnic groups, the war in Europe evoked feelings of rage and a strong desire to do something to help, even if it was only a symbolic act designed to rouse public consciousness. The *Dal*, a one-masted sloop on which a pair of Poles fled across the Atlantic, was presented with great ceremony to the Museum of Science and Industry. Polish refugees occupied a once-abandoned house at Milwaukee Avenue and Throop Street, established as a hostel by the Polish Roman Catholic Union and furnished with donations from the neighborhood.[99]

The tragedy of the war struck no group harder than Chicago's Jewish community. As news filtered to America about Jews being murdered in Europe, Chicago's Jewish community roused public sentiments to support rescue efforts. Mass meetings in March and April 1943 told of the two million Jews already dead and the five million in peril. On April 14, 1943, twenty thousand people jammed Chicago Stadium to hear political and religious leaders explain efforts to approach the German government through neutral countries and of the efforts to alter American immigration laws to facilitate Jewish refugees' escape. Chicago's Jewry, along with religious leaders and laypersons from a wide cross section of the city, created the Emergency Committee to Save the Jewish People of Europe. This group advocated the creation of a federal agency to aid Jews escaping from Axis satellite countries through neutral countries. They argued that the establishment of a specific agency would indicate to Nazi-controlled countries that the United States was determined to end the extermination of the Jews.[100]

Wartime and Minority Tensions

Chicago's function as an urban crossroads meant that different ethnic and racial groups competed for living space. One of those was the black community. Located on the South Side, it was as old as the city itself. Its residents had been left devastated by the Great Depression and largely denied a share of the recovery.[101] They constituted nearly two-thirds of those still on relief at the beginning of the war, although they made up less than 10 percent of the population. Discrimination meant that they paid 3 percent more for food; OPA investigations found heavy concentrations of price-control violators in their neighborhoods.[102] Moreover, few African-Americans found their neighborhoods to be nurturing

environments. In December 1941, for instance, nearly all of the Chicago public schools that held only half-day classes because of overcrowding were located in black residential areas.[103]

Margaret East crocheted a large American flag in 1944 while riding the elevated trains to work each day. In an article in the *Chicago Defender*, East told reporters that she regularly corresponded with several men in the service to keep their spirits up.

The *Chicago Defender* publicized Dorie Miller's heroic actions at Pearl Harbor at a time when African-Americans were usually relegated to menial positions in the military. In addition to fighting the Axis powers, African-Americans continued their struggle against racial discrimination on the homefront. The war often heightened racial tension, especially in the areas of housing and employment.

Employment prospects improved dramatically during the war, but, some claimed, the quality of life deteriorated for many black Chicagoans, in large part, because the prospect of defense jobs triggered the immigration of sixty-five thousand additional people into a district whose boundaries were not allowed to grow. The influx had begun late in the 1930s, when northern factories began to produce war goods. Living spaces got more crowded each year.[104] In 1943 Robert Taylor of the Chicago Housing Authority noted that the population density of ninety thousand persons per square mile was greater than that of the slums of Calcutta.

Faced with nowhere else to go, black Chicagoans paid rents that were 25 percent higher for apartments that were almost always smaller and more deteriorated than those in white neighborhoods.[105] One city welfare administration report described the plight of one family: "Mrs. X has five children. . . . Her husband, a G.I., has been returned from overseas service for hospitalization. The family occupies an unheated three-room apartment. . . . [Rats] race around the apartment day and night. . . . The baby has had his nose entirely bitten off by rats, his entire body lacerated. His mother was awakened at 4 A.M. to find the child almost smothered by the rodents."[106]

These conditions at home were matched by the blatant discrimination encountered in the military, where African-Americans were segregated and trained for menial tasks. Many were stunned to learn that their blood was segregated by the American Red Cross, even though a black doctor, Charles L. Drew, had played a leading role in establishing the blood bank system. The Red Cross claimed it was merely following military policy. All of this produced a widespread sense of dismay and anger in black Chicagoans.

Their most potent weapon was the power of publicity. Although the *Chicago Defender* promoted a generalized protest known as the "Double-V" campaign—victory at home as well as abroad—the press was most effective when focused on a specific issue, such as the case of Dorie Miller. Although never taught how to fire a machine gun, the black messman on the battleship *Arizona* seized one during the Pearl Harbor bombing and shot down four Japanese planes. The navy, whose policies relegated minorities to the status of servants, at first refused to recognize Miller's heroism, but relented after a campaign led by the *Defender* and awarded him the Navy Cross.[107]

The fact that African-Americans' living conditions deteriorated, while their wages went up, during the war attracted little public attention in the white community until 1943. The Detroit and Harlem race riots of the summer of 1943, which caused widespread death and destruction, frightened Chicago officials. Initially, Mayor Kelly tried to ignore the events, telling reporters, "There is no race trouble in Chicago."[108] Within days, however, Kelly shifted his approach completely. He quickly pushed a bill through the City Council, establishing the Mayor's Committee on Race Relations. Composed of six white and five black civic leaders, it called for calm and understanding and tried to educate the public about the need to control vicious rumors. Some community leaders labeled the committee a hollow gesture, but Kelly, who was enormously popular on the South Side, had equally vocal supporters.[109] He transformed the committee into a permanent city department. Its executive director, economist Robert C. Weaver, convinced police officials to formulate a plan to prevent small incidents from growing into riots. The strategy worked, and Chicago avoided violence.[110]

Japanese-Americans

The arrival of thousands of relocated Japanese-Americans in Chicago also became a convenient opportunity to reduce direct racial conflict at a time when tensions were growing within the black community. On December 7, 1941, Chicago's Japanese community consisted of about 350 people, most of whom were scattered across the city rather than concentrated in one neighborhood.

The public response to the Japanese presence in the months that followed the "Day of Infamy" fit no particular pattern. Samuel I. Hayakawa, a thirty-six-year-old English literature professor at Illinois Institute of Technology, reported that "Not once since Pearl Harbor have I been subjected to any annoying experiences. I have ridden busses, streetcars and taxis and never have been the target of any remark."[111] Others were not as fortunate, especially during the first part of the war. One Japanese-American committed suicide in June 1942 after he was denied a job because of his ancestry.

Many other Asian Chicagoans feared being mistaken for Japanese. Pamphlets and magazine articles attempted to describe the physical differences, and some Chinese wore buttons proclaiming their ancestry as a defense against discrimination. Similar identity problems plagued the Filipino community, numbering as many as four thousand and centered around LaSalle Street and Chicago Avenue on the North Side. "Don't stare rudely at the dark-skinned little man who passes you on the street," commented *Daily News* columnist Sydney J. Harris two weeks after Pearl Harbor, "He is most likely a loyal Filipino who is aching to get at the Japs as much as any other American citizen." The Filipino National Council, located in Chicago, distributed buttons with the words "Filipino—U.S.A." to more than thirty-five thousand of their compatriots

Chiye Tomihiro
I'd like to talk about the psychological aspect of [the internment and relocation of Japanese-Americans]. When I came here people would always ask me where I was from, naturally thinking that I was going to say I was either from China or whatever. And when I'd say that I was from Portland, Oregon, they invariably asked me "why would you want to live in Chicago?... Portland is such a beautiful place!" And do you know, I could not tell them why! I couldn't tell them I had been evacuated, I had been put in camp, and I was forced to leave Portland.... I shouldn't have been ashamed, but I was. It wasn't until the commission had their hearings, the Commission on Relocation and Internment of Civilians had their hearings here in Chicago in September of 1981, that I confronted all of this for the first time.

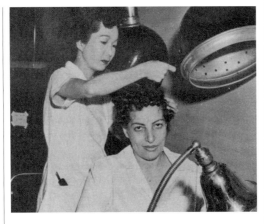

Above, Japanese-Americans were allowed to leave wartime detention camps in the western states such as this one in Manzanar, California, if they could secure employment inland. Over twenty thousand Japanese-Americans eventually relocated in Chicago where they struggled to reestablish their lives and create a new community.

centers in early 1942. On June 12 of that year, the first evacuees from the camps arrived in Chicago, and within six months the city had become their most concentrated destination. By mid-1944 arrivals had reached the rate of twenty-five a day, and the community reached over fifty-one hundred. Ultimately, some twenty thousand relocated evacuees arrived, and because San Francisco and Los Angeles had been virtually depopulated by camp relocation, Chicago's Japanese community became the largest in the nation.[114]

The choice of Chicago was logical. As the war progressed, the labor shortage in the city worsened, and although Japanese-Americans were considered unsuitable for defense industry jobs, many evacuees quickly found employment in the service industry. Others used their skills in printing plants, food processing industries, secretarial work, and suburban nurseries. Noting that 85 percent of those coming to Chicago were young, Harold Jacoby of the War Relocation Authority (WRA) observed, "These young people won't slave in a truck field for a diet of rice as their parents did, but will demand the kind of pay their white co-workers are getting."[115] But the reality was often quite different. One man described the young maids at the Edgewater Beach Hotel: "The hotel work is too hard. . . . In fact, they are losing weight and one girl became sick from overwork. They have to clean about fifteen suites a day, scrubbing the floors on their hands and knees."[116]

The growing Japanese-American community also attracted lawyers and doctors, as well as businesspeople, who opened restaurants, food stores, recreation and pool halls, and rooming houses. The relative lack of hostility—one government publication called it a "cloak of indifference"—also made it much easier to find housing for the evacuees. Initially, the WRA wanted to avoid the creation

scattered across the country.[112] There were a few other incidents. The Japanese Tea House in Jackson Park was torn down in July 1942 on orders of federal customs officials, for fear that "some patriotic person would set fire to it." As the war continued, the Japanese garden that surrounded it was vandalized.[113]

Despite these incidents and the common use of the word "Jap" in the press, Japanese-Americans were far luckier to be in Chicago than along the Pacific Coast, from which thousands were removed to the desert internment

The neighborhood was the backbone of the civilian war effort, linking the individual household and the citywide civilian defense program. The neighborhood was the most important mass educator of families, providing information about how to be both prepared and patriotic. The neighborhood also shouldered the burden of explaining a maze of new regulations to bewildered consumers.

The flow of intelligence also went the other direction. The war emergency mandated that neighborhood officials invade the privacy of the family to collect detailed information about the daily habits of citizens. Who they were, where they worked, what hours they kept, how many cans of tomatoes they had in their pantry, how many scrap tires were in the garage—such information ended up in a block captain's files.

The neighborhood also functioned as a substitute for some of the normal aspects of family life that the war had removed. Patriotic activity groups and block captains often became surrogate parents in place of those who were away at work or in the service. The victory garden was the critical neighborhood replacement for fruits and vegetables that were in short supply.

of a "Little Tokyo" and carefully scattered the first arrivals across the city. Clustering aided adjustment, however, and by late in the war two Japanese-American neighborhoods had begun to emerge. One was centered at Clark and Division streets on the North Side, where by 1947 evacuees operated forty-two businesses. The other was in the Kenwood-Oakenwald section of the South Side, east of Cottage Grove Avenue between Forty-third and Forty-seventh streets.[117]

The location of the two Japanese-American communities was significant, in large part because they functioned as buffer zones. On one side of each was an affluent white neighborhood, Hyde Park on the South Side and the Gold Coast on the North Side. On the other side of each was a run-down area that was marked, in the words of a Chicago Resettlers Committee report, by "the over-flowing Negro districts and the receding white neighborhoods."[118] Federal housing policy at that time did not encourage racial integration, while real estate interests were prejudiced against the evacuees and convinced that, in the words of one realtor, "wherever they locate, rentals and property values toboggan."[119]

Below, a company service flag hangs from International Harvester's headquarters on Michigan Avenue. Such flags reinforced the sense of community in the workplace and the human contribution of companies in support of the war effort: 15,264 workers were in active service, sixty-three of whom died.

Relocated Japanese-Americans faced the problem of creating instant communities in areas that were not entirely of their choice. Yet, at the same time, any institution-building on their part might have aroused a negative reaction among more xenophobic Chicagoans. Finally, black neighborhoods grew so rapidly in population without expanding geographically that increasing numbers of their people perceived them as traps, rather than nurturing environments.

The last two years of the war proved to be very different from the first two. Rationing and shortages wore down the patience of consumers. More families had loved ones on the battlefield. The passing months also made it difficult to sustain the enthusiasm of civilian defense as a protective organization. But the last years also saw increasing tension on the neighborhood level as well.

What held this diverse city together? Unity was achieved through two means in peacetime. Civic patriotism in the form of flags, symbols, historical accounts of the city's rise to greatness, and other local parallels to nationalism unified diverse Chicagoans. The Democratic machine helped unify a variety of ethnic groups, the business community, and organized labor into a powerful coalition. During the war, the civilian defense effort assumed the responsibility of attempting to unify the city's diverse people toward a common goal of American victory.

A young boy poses next to an elaborate neighborhood honor roll that stood at 2100 West Addison. Pictures and addresses identified the men and women from the block who were in military service. The three pictures in gold stars above the eagle identify those who died in service.

The ideal neighborhood structure that had been created around civilian defense faced a series of challenges. One was the difficulty of maintaining a sense of unity among the diverse collection of inward-looking, tightly knit neighborhoods. Clearly, the war meant different things to different ethnic and racial groups. European groups were emotionally tied to the conflicts involving their homelands.

Previous page: Chicago artist Samuel Greenburg submitted this poster design to a competition sponsored by The Art Institute of Chicago in 1942. It was one of four posters purchased by Chicago's Office of Civilian Defense.

Right, *Furlough's End* by Samuel Greenburg. Oil on canvas, c. 1943.

Cover from the 1945 Chicago Telephone
Book, which depicts the city's importance
as a crossroads for the nation.

Above, this bleak scene of the detention camp at Gila River, Arizona, was painted by Shozaburo Otani, a Japanese-American man who was interned at the camp. Many internees took up arts and crafts to pass the time and help them deal with the difficulty of being forced into detention camps.

Right, this powerful British poster, which was distributed in the United States, stresses the danger of internal sabotage.

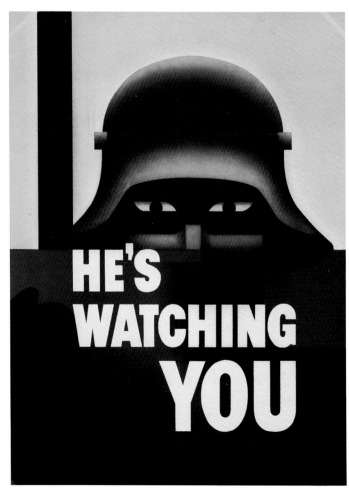

HE'S WATCHING YOU

Hundreds of posters such as this one urged Americans to buy war bonds to help finance the war.

BUY WAR BONDS

Children contributed to the homefront effort in many ways, including collecting scrap materials that could be recycled into defense goods.

WE'RE SCRAPPERS TOO

Above, this deck of Vargas girls playing cards had a military theme.

Left, children's wartime toys idealized military personnel. In addition, most toys, such as these paper dolls, were made out of nonvital materials.

I AM INVESTING 10% OR MORE IN WAR BONDS

WE'RE BUYING AT LEAST 10%

MEMBER · Dr Scholl's 5th WAR BOND DRIVE

"THIS IS MY FIGHT TOO!"

PUT AT LEAST 10% EVERY PAYDAY IN WAR BONDS

Winning the production war at home was vital to winning the war overseas. Chicagoans were encouraged not only to work long hours, but also to invest their earnings in war bonds. Opposite, a poster by Jean Carlu conveys the confidence many had in America's industries.

The Production War

On December 16, 1944, the eyes of Chicago looked up toward a giant airplane that circled the city for over an hour before landing at Municipal (now Midway) Airport for a public inspection. The flight of the new B-29 bomber had double significance for Chicagoans that day. Not only did they finally get to see the superweapon that the military claimed would bring victory over the Axis, but the flight was a point of pride for the fifty local companies that had manufactured parts. Over half of the plane, by weight, originated as aluminum sheeting from ALCOA in suburban McCook. Dodge-Chicago, the sprawling complex on South Cicero Avenue, had constructed its four eighteen-cylinder, twenty-two-hundred horse-power Wright Cyclone engines. The nose frame, electrical assembly, guns, bomb bay doors, oxygen equipment, and automatic pilot had all come from area companies. The B-29 may have been assembled elsewhere, but Chicagoans thought of it as their plane.[1]

By the time the B-29 made its flight over Chicago, only Detroit was producing war goods of greater dollar value. By mid-1944, war contracts within the city had reached $7.8 billion of the total $23 billion in the Chicago Ordnance District, which included the northern parts of Illinois and Indiana, as well as Iowa, Wisconsin, and Minnesota. At that point, total domestic expenditures had reached $195.1 billion. In 1944 alone, the Chicago region produced $10.4 billion in goods and services sold to military procurement agencies. More than 74 percent of the production in the Chicago Ordnance District was classified as "critical" to the war effort.[2]

Chicago's industrial life was dramatically reordered during World War II. The entire economic life of the community was both revived and interrupted by the national need for supplies. Where some $2 billion in orders were being filled early in 1942, expenditures had been virtually zero in 1939, the year that a three-man staff—the sum total of personnel in the entire Chicago Ordnance District until November 1940—began to update a twenty-year-old survey of the manufacturing capabilities of each of the thousands of companies under its jurisdiction.[3] The war touched all of Chicago's manufacturers. Even those that did not change what they manufactured faced supply shortages, transportation difficulties, price ceilings, and rationed or banned sales.

GIVE 'EM
BOTH BARRELS

Top, this poster by Jean Carlu depicts the American industrial worker as the soldier of the homefront. Above right, this pin from the Hawthorne works of Western Electric in Cicero bears a "Minute Man" designation, meaning that 90 percent of the employees participated in the seventh war bond drive.

The story of the war industry in Chicago also reaches into the neighborhood and the individual home. The factory caused many social changes in the home. Defense jobs drew thousands of workers to Chicago, creating a housing shortage, while new factory construction and increased job opportunities drew workers further away from their homes and neighborhoods than ever before. Among these workers were tens of thousands of women, who joined the work force in unprecedented numbers. Factory schedules reached into the household, forcing families to shift their schedules. Industrial plants lured high school dropouts who could not get into the military. And smokestacks spewed a choking reminder that Chicago was America's arsenal.

Cutting the Pattern

The enormity of Chicago's contribution to America's defense industries and the compressed time in which it all took place gave the appearance of controlled chaos. Issue after issue of *Chicago Commerce*, the Chamber of Commerce and Industry journal, and the real estate chronicle, *The Economist*, listed new factories, moves to larger facilities, additions made to old ones, and new products. From June 1940 through V-J Day, private companies and the federal War Plant Corporation, which built and leased some of the larger factory spaces, spent $1.3 billion in factory construction, a third of it invested in over three hundred new buildings.[4] At no time in the city's history had there been industrial investment of such magnitude in so short a time. But the defense boom was anything but illogical in the way it was planned. Under the direction of former Sears, Roebuck executive Donald Nelson, the federal War Production Board (WPB) employed a series of tactics that used both inducements and coercion to obtain the vast array of required military equipment.[5]

While the need to conserve precious materials justified the orders halting the manufacture of some six hundred consumer products during the first two months of the war, those edicts left many companies with idle production capacity. Faced with the prospect of a complete shutdown and the loss of key personnel, most manufacturers were only too happy to bid on defense contracts. The result was often a curious change in products that contrasted the innocence of civilian life with the reality of war. The Chicago Roller Skate Company turned out nose sections of bombers and small parts for shells and guns, while the manufacturer of Radio Flyer wagons modified its stamping machines to fashion five-gallon gasoline "blitz cans." Vaughn

Manufacturing Company turned from can and bottle openers to bomb fuzes, and Rock-ola, the giant jukebox manufacturer, produced 30-mm M-1 carbine rifles.[6]

Government-sponsored seminars and information packets aided the bidding process by explaining specifications in detail, which helped companies seeking contracts based on what they already did, or what they thought they could most easily retool to do. Some manufacturers overestimated their abilities, but simply had no choice other than to take what was available. Investments in new machine tools and plant capacity often ate up any windfall profit they might have realized. Ekco Products, for instance, discovered that there

were great differences between making tinware and stainless steel kitchen utensils with 250-ton metal presses and making navy shell casings with two-thousand-ton presses. The company had to construct new buildings around new machinery and create a new metallurgy laboratory as well.[7]

The encouragement of subcontracting also aided the conversion of plants. Early in the conflict, the WPB usually chose a single contractor to make all of the parts for, as well as assemble, a particular product. One local WPB official defended this policy: "Winning the war is more important than spreading the burden more equitably."[8] But political pressure, including that applied by Mayor Kelly, along with complaints from small business associations, pushed military purchase agents toward a broadening of industrial involvement.[9] At the same time, the growing complexity of weapons systems meant a decreased likelihood that any but the largest firms had the full range of needed equipment and talent. As a result, officials of the Chicago Ordnance District, which coordinated weapons procurement, and the companies themselves chose to distribute the contracts for component parts among a number of subcontractors, and then bring all of the pieces together in one place for final assembly.[10]

The subcontracting system offered several advantages. It distributed defense contracts to many small firms, considerably boosting morale by allowing more companies

The Norden bombsight (left) was a closely kept military secret. Although not all factories produced such top-secret equipment, workers were strongly discouraged from discussing their work for fear that any information would aid the enemy (above).

Military rations made by Kraft Foods. Chicago possessed the nation's largest concentration of food-processing equipment. Of all major cities, it was most capable of filling the huge orders for military rations.

to profit. Secondly, contracts for small elements such as springs, knobs, bearings, and castings of various sizes allowed smaller companies to utilize existing equipment and workers because these items were often similar to what they already manufactured. Since no one knew how long the war and the contracts would last, corporations naturally wanted to minimize their investment. Subcontracting also required a shorter start-up time, especially in a metropolitan area the size of Chicago, where the larger scale and diversity of the local economy guaranteed a greater range of specialized suppliers that could handle part and sub-assembly work. In other words, the subdivision of production worked well in a big city.[11]

Finally, the dispersal of manufacturing contracts made it easier to conceal the true nature of many of the weapons under development or details about existing ones. Government officials claimed that Nazi espionage agents were constantly attempting to penetrate defense plants across the country. In the most famous local case, Herbert Haupt, the lens-grinder-turned-saboteur, was captured as he was about to return to his job at Chicago's Simpson Optical Company, which made parts for the top-secret Norden bombsight. The tightest security was reserved for the major assembly points. Thus, many Chicago workers labored for four years, producing individual components without ever knowing their purpose.[12]

Building on History

Initially, war contracts flowed into Chicago at an excruciatingly slow rate. Mayor Kelly and delegations from the Chicago Association of Commerce and Industry made many trips to Washington during 1941 and 1942 in an effort to divert some of the defense business away from the coasts. Over 350 individual companies dispatched their own representatives, some of whom distributed colorful promotional brochures describing facilities and personnel to the army and navy procurement departments. Lt. Gen. William S. Knudsen, director of production for the War Department and former General Motors president, applauded Chicago's self-promotion: "The thing that has really impressed me most in Chicago has been everybody saying, 'What do you want? We can take more.'"[13] This intensive lobbying, along with the fear of enemy coastal attack, helped shift war contracts inland, especially to the major Great Lakes industrial belt dominated by Chicago and Detroit. On March 20, 1942, the air force opened a local procurement office.[14] The idle factories of early 1942 were soon a memory, and in less than two years Chicago became one of the nation's leading arsenals.

Chicago's industrial prominence during World War II grew out of its history. Its location in the Midwest farm country gave it a great advantage in bidding for military food contracts. Chicago possessed the nation's largest concentration of food-processing machinery. It was America's baking and candy-making center, and it turned out more processed meats than any other city. Of all major cities, it was most capable of filling the huge orders for military rations. Chicago's agglomeration of producers, in turn, increased transportation efficiency because of its proximity to the Quartermaster's Corps' acquisition center and warehouse, which was set up in the Central Manufacturing District. It also increased the efficiency of military food inspectors, who had to travel only a few miles to do much of their work.[15]

With the exception of candy and gum, nearly all of which went to the military, foodstuffs were processed to save weight and space and to survive extremes of temperature and a long shelf life. Many companies devel-

oped new processes in cooperation with the Quartermaster's Corps' subsistence research and development laboratory located in Chicago.[16] Kraft Foods introduced a line of cheeses in tins.[17] Low-bulk, high-energy foods, however, made up most of the local production. Cracker-Jack, for instance, created a separate three-thousand-calorie K-Ration unit for breakfast, lunch, and dinner. Each contained a combination of items such as crackers, meat, cheese, candy, gum, and, in powdered form, juice, bouillon, and coffee.[18]

Chicago's clothing industry also mobilized for the war. A few local companies turned out uniforms, carrying on the city's tradition of garment manufacture that had thrived for decades. Most wartime textile-related contracts, however, came from the conversion of facilities that made fabric products of similar size. Bearse Manufacturing Company, which normally produced coated cloth bags of various types, turned over all of its production to bomb tail covers, barracks bags, gun slings, and mosquito netting. Several companies manufactured parachute equipment. The textile factories owned by Marshall Field & Co. man-

Above, the Wrigley Company shifted all of its gum production to the military. Left, sales display for a Kraft Foods "chow kit", which could be purchased and mailed to service personnel.

ufactured parachute and tenting cloth, while its lace factory in north suburban Zion made miles of mosquito netting.[19]

The production of basic metals, perhaps the most vital of all war industries, flourished in Chicago because of the traditional power of location. Iron and steel furnaces had enjoyed easy access to raw materials from the northern Great Lakes ore fields and efficient distribution through the railway network. Most companies had taken advantage of the economic revival of the late 1930s to modernize their plants, especially in the Calumet region of Indiana. Even with expansion, Chicago-area mills, which had operated at only 36 percent capacity in 1938 exceeded 100 percent by the end of 1942. At the vast works of Carnegie-Illinois Steel in Gary, Indiana, twenty-three thousand workers operating fifty-three open hearth and twelve blast furnaces in the spring of 1943 produced more than the total output of Japan.[20] On October 29, 1942, American Steel Foundries opened the largest plant ever built for the production of cast armor plate.[21]

The lack of space limited the expansion plans of the steel industry within the city itself, but midway through 1944 Republic Steel opened a new plant at 116th and Burley streets. This facility used electric furnaces, in part because they eliminated the need to haul cars of coals and ashes in and out of the plant, but also because electricity was so abundant in the region.[22] That energy resource was also the main reason that the WPB chose suburban McCook over Los Angeles as the site of a major rolling mill for the Aluminum Company of America. Inside the main building, which was bigger than forty-two football fields, bauxite ore became three-thousand-pound ingots, then flat sheets more than a city block long, and finally the skin of thousands of war planes.[23]

The Assembled War

World War II demonstrated the degree to which military weapons had evolved from large and simple machinery, often cast in a single piece in an armory, to smaller complex devices made almost entirely by private industry. Traditional warfare had become an assembled war. The Norden bombsight, whose pinpoint accuracy gave the Allies a decided edge in one phase of aerial warfare, comprised hundreds of tiny precision pieces. These and thousands of other war goods were a testament to American skill in design and fabrication.

The more complicated the military hardware, the less chance that any one manufacturer could make all of the parts. The fragmentation of production that resulted paralleled the government's policy of contract dispersal. In turn, this tendency toward dispersal made large cities all the more important because of the agglomeration of specialized skills that always existed in urban areas. Chicago rose to industrial prominence in the nineteenth century less through the simple production of primary metals than through the skills its factories mastered to fabricate that metal into a wide variety of products for both consumers and other producers. Thus, when military procurement agencies sought contractors for a wide array of goods, northeastern Illinois companies could supply virtually anything, often without even modifying their existing machines.

Much of the heavy industry in earlier decades had involved cutting, bending, and otherwise shaping heavy sheet steel into equipment that operated out of America's transportation hub. That technology translated easily into heavy military equipment. While many Great Lakes companies had more wooden ship–building experience, Pullman-Standard knew how to bend heavy metal. It converted part of its railroad car–building plant to the production of subchasers, launch-

ing its first vessel on Lake Calumet on May 2, 1943, and its first Landing Ship Medium (LSM) on April 29, 1944. Pullman, however, did not halt its rail car production completely. During the war, it also made fifty railway hospital cars and sixteen hundred troop sleepers, each of which could accommodate thirty men in wide seats and triple-decker bunks. In addition, American Car and Foundry built freight cars and wheels, as well as troop kitchen cars at its Chicago plant.[24]

The skill of shaping heavy metal vehicles also helped make Chicago one of the nation's leading tank production centers. Instead of the usual freight cars, the assembly lines at Pressed Steel Car Company's Hegewisch plant rolled out 10,750 armored vehicles, including the M-4 "Sherman" medium tanks, the M-12 "Long Tom," the Scorpion mine destroyer, and the M7B1 "Tank Buster."[25]

Above, Goss Printing manufactured naval guns during the war. Opposite top, factory security badges. Workers' identification badges were among the security measures implemented by factories during the war. Opposite below, a scene from the Dodge-Chicago plant shows metal casting for airplane engines.

Top, Schwinn Bicycle Co. used their metal bending and welding equipment to make a myriad of small components used in defense projects. Above, International Harvester's Tractor Works manufactured farm tractors and related equipment for the war effort.

Some heavy equipment companies, especially those that supplied producer goods, were fortunate because they needed only minor retooling and could sell virtually all of their output to the military. Marketing and advertising became unnecessary except to generate public goodwill and to hold the company's place in the domestic market. Barber-Greene and Austin-Western made graders and other road construction equip-

ment for the Army Corps of Engineers and Seabees instead of local governments. The conversion to diesel ship engine manufacture required few modifications for the General Motors Electro-Motive Division plant in suburban LaGrange. These engines were virtually identical to those that powered the giant diesel-electric railroad locomotives that the company continued to build.[26]

Decades of peacetime production had given Chicago companies the skill to stamp, drill, and machine steel into almost any shape. Chicago's economy had grown to industrial maturity at a time when steel had gradually made its way into many consumer items that had once been made of wood, glass, or cast iron. This included, for instance, two of the nation's largest gas range makers, American Stove and Cribben & Sexton (Universal). Those who made domestic items with flat surfaces, such as kitchen appliances and metal cabinets, ended up making some of the multitudinous cases needed to house military gear, radio equipment, and shells. Companies experienced in bent tubing products had the most success making items such as portable shower systems and gasoline filler spouts for military vehicles. The National Mineral Company, now Helene Curtis, changed over from the production of beauty salon hair dryers to antennas. The Arnold, Schwinn Bicycle Company made similar use of its bent tube skills.[27]

The military's greatest need, however, was for weaponry of all types and sizes. Shells and bullets were as much a military consumable as food, and the expansion of America's fighting forces throughout the war and the loss of equipment in battle meant that demand was constantly increasing. Army and navy officials never ceased telling Chicagoans and the rest of the nation that shortages hampered progress toward an earlier victory.

What various companies could contribute to this effort again depended largely on what prewar experience had taught them. The production of pumps at the Hannifan Manufacturing Company involved pneumatic and hydraulic systems with pistons and close bores inside of tubes; during the war they made 75-mm Howitzers and recoil mechanisms for large guns. At the other extreme were makers of precision goods and jewelry such as F. H. Noble on the Southwest Side and the Elgin Watch Company in the northwest suburbs, both of which constructed delicate parts for fuzes that timed the explosion of shells of all sizes. Dozens of companies made gun magazines, shell and bullet links, gun carriages, aerial bombs, hand grenades, and other ordnance.[28]

The most complex piece of World War II ammunition was the torpedo, a self-propelled "thinking" weapon. It took over twenty thousand separate work operations to make its five thousand parts, some of them machined down to twenty-five millionths of an inch and requiring large magnifying glasses to assemble. And at ten thousand dollars each, the torpedo was easily the most expensive "bullet," but its ability to sink an $80 million enemy ship made it a bargain. Two Chicago plants made complete torpedoes. The McCormick Reaper Works of International Harvester, a century-old manufacturer of farm implements, set aside two thousand of its employees and a seven-story plant to make "tin fish." Amertorp Corporation, a new seventeen-acre facility in Forest Park, was jointly developed by the navy and the American Can Company.[29]

The ultimate product of the "assembled war" was the airplane. Despite Chicago's enthusiasm for flying and the emergence of Municipal Airport as the nation's busiest air transportation hub, the city had enjoyed few of the benefits of the rise of the aircraft industry. Chicago seemed destined to load and unload planes made elsewhere. Only a few small manufacturers had appeared on the outskirts of the city.[30]

Above, workers at Douglas-Chicago in Park Ridge assemble a C-54 Skymaster. The Austin Co. built the world's largest all-timber factory for Douglas-Chicago.

WRIGHT CYCLONE 18BA (R3350BA) SERIES AIRCRAFT ENGINE
Exploded View of a Typical Engine

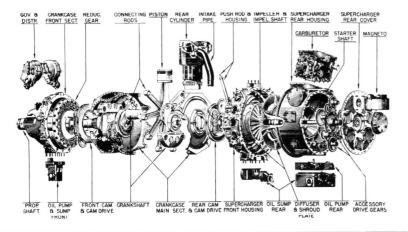

For a few years, however, Chicago was an important aircraft production center. The threat of Japanese bombing made federal officials and industry leaders nervous about the security of plants in California, while the need for rapid expansion exceeded the resources available on the West Coast and other aircraft centers. Although some manufacturers, including Douglas, erected plants on the plains of Kansas, the availability of land and labor in Chicago attracted many manufacturers. But Chicago's main lure was its enormous capacity to produce the thousands of machined parts necessary to construct a plane.[31]

Chicago's wartime emergence as an aircraft manufacturing center progressed through three stages. As late as early 1941, its role had been limited to the production of metals, instruments, cable, and felt. By mid-1942, two hundred Chicago-area factories supplied a wide variety of these simple components.[32] Walmark Manufacturing in Downers Grove made carburetor parts for giant Bendix Aviation.[33] On a much larger scale, the Studebaker Company opened a new plant at Fifty-fifth, Cicero, and Archer, adjacent to Municipal Airport, in February 1942. Its fifty-nine hundred employees cast and machined major magnesium parts for the nine-cylinder Wright Cyclone engine. Trucks and rail cars carried these components to South Bend for final assembly.[34]

The second stage involved the assembly of major components, which was probably the region's greatest contribution to the air war. Two major aircraft engine manufacturers erected huge plants on the city's outskirts. On March 17, 1941, the Buick division of General Motors broke ground for a $31 million plant at a 125-acre site on North Avenue in Melrose Park. In September it began producing twelve-hundred horsepower Pratt and

Whitney engines for Liberator bombers, which were assembled at the Ford Motor Company's Willow Run plant near Detroit. By the following June, Harlow Curtice, Buick's president, was so pleased that the new plant was running far ahead of output schedules that he predicted that Chicago would become the nation's center of aircraft engine production.[35]

While Curtice was extolling the virtues of Chicago, Chrysler Corporation was breaking ground for its new $110 million Dodge-Chicago engine plant on the South Side. This plant was to be larger than Buick and Studebaker combined; at the time it was hailed as the biggest industrial plant ever constructed. When finally completed in January 1944, its thirty-two thousand workers took only fifteen months to produce ten thousand B-29 engines.[36]

The final stage of production was the assembly of the entire plane. Although not the largest plant, the Douglas-Chicago facility in Park Ridge symbolized the most complex achievement of Chicago industry during the war. The building itself was unusual because it was made almost entirely of wood. Only the pipes were steel, thus saving some thirty thousand tons of critical metals for other defense uses.[37] On March 31, 1943, the plant was dedicated as a C-54 Skymaster, the craft that would soon be built there, landed at the adja-

cent airport. Chicagoans were astounded by the aircraft's size. It was one of the largest planes built and was destined to become the cargo workhorse of the war.[38]

The speed with which the new plant assembled its first plane is another example of how the war compressed time. The company had been hiring and training workers for nearly a year, which minimized the start-up time. In addition, everything that was constructed outside of the building was made by nearby subcontractors. The engines came from Buick in Melrose Park, while some wing assemblies came from Pullman-Standard. Less-than-subtle coaxing helped as well. Everywhere workers turned they saw the "Fly in July" slogan—on clocks, posters, giant banners, and a fifteen-foot high "thermometer" that measured progress.[39]

On July 30 the company achieved its goal when the *Chicago* roared down the runway in front of fifty thousand onlookers. Amidst the speechmaking at the ceremony, a Douglas vice president commented, "Some day we will turn again to the ways of peace. Then, as now, it will be good common sense to choose Chicago, the geographic and economic transportation center of the North American continent, as the center for the production of this and other transport aircraft to follow."[40]

Opposite above, workers construct aircraft engines at Studebaker's Chicago Aviation Plant. Various Chicago factories manufactured components for C-47 model transport planes (above), but the Douglas-Chicago plant assembled the plane itself. Opposite below, an exploded view of a B-29 airplane engine, which was made at the Dodge-Chicago plant. Each twenty-two-hundred horsepower engine weighed 2,670 pounds. Four such engines powered each B-29 "Superfortress."

New Frontiers

The creation of something as complex as a cargo plane demonstrated the degree to which World War II was a research war. It was the first modern technological conflict where combatants were driven by a need to make improvements to existing products. Politicians loved to tell constituents that "soldiers without guns" were as important as those on the battlefields. According to them, workers in laboratories, defense factories, and the local USO were all soldiers.

Chicago's role in national defense production mirrored its emergence during the early twentieth century as the city with the largest concentration of industries based on new products and manufacturing processes. In other words, Chicago functioned as the nation's center for what we now call high-tech industry. Electronics, along with the internal combustion engine, formed the heart of these new advances during the first four decades of the century.

Electronics developed beyond simple wiring and switching devices, although manufacture of those items continued. The new frontier of research was in electronic controls. The Powers Regulator Company, a thermostat manufacturer, made a wide variety of temperature controls, gauges, and recorders for weapons equipment, as well as control panels. A competitor, Minneapolis-Honeywell, established a Chicago branch during the war, ostensibly to build pneumatic control systems. What it actually built, however, was a new electronic autopilot, which was a military secret until September 1943. Standard equipment in all American heavy bombers, it permitted remote-control operation at two or more places in a plane, so that crews could navigate even after manual controls had been shot away.[41]

The Chicago area also had the largest concentration of communications device manufacturers. The largest was Western Electric, part of the Bell System; its mammoth plant straddled the Chicago-Cicero border. When radio crackled into popularity after World War I, Chicago became the nation's largest single radio manufacturing center, with over forty producers on the eve of the war, including such giants as Majestic, Galvin (Motorola), Zenith, Hallicrafters, and Webster-Chicago (Webcor), the latter also the nation's leading manufacturer of automatic phonographs. This new industry needed room to expand, ready transportation access to raw materials and shipment of finished products, and a large labor force. These requirements were met in Chicago, where procurement officers purchased approximately half of all military electronics needs during the war.[42]

At first, radio companies converted available products to serve basic communications needs, but it was soon obvious that extensive retooling was necessary. And while that was in

Citizens were encouraged to buy bonds to invest in a future filled with lifestyle-improving technologies.

He gets and gives orders by RADIO

1917 WAR RUN BY TELEPHONE

1943 WAR RUN BY RADIO

ZENITH LONG DISTANCE RADIO

RADIONIC PRODUCTS EXCLUSIVELY—
WORLD'S LEADING MANUFACTURER

BETTER THAN CASH—U. S. WAR SAVINGS STAMPS AND BONDS

radar to detonate a bomb or rocket at a pre-determined distance from its target. This was the "smart bomb" of its day.[43]

Radar aside, no war product captured the public's fascination as much as the walkie-talkie. The original Handie-Talkie was invent-ed by the Galvin Corporation's chief engi-neer, Donald H. Mitchell, early in the war. "When I saw the heavy cumbersome field radios used," he later recalled, "I [said] 'That's no kind of equipment with which to fight a war.' . . . They were using radios which took two men to handle—equipment of the type used in World War I." Mitchell miniaturized everything into a five-and-one-half pound waterproof transmitter-receiver containing 585 parts and powered by only two small batteries. Nothing before or since has so revolutionized battlefield communications, and few items drew as many crowds at department store dis-plays and military production exhibitions.[44]

Also unique about Chicago's communi-cations manufacturers was their willingness to cooperate. No other industry created a trade organization as powerful as the Radar-Radio Industries of Chicago, Incorporated. By July 1944 it had sixty-three member firms, which em-ployed over forty thousand workers who turned out over 50 percent of all electronics equipment produced in the United States.[45]

The atmosphere of wartime urgency also helped catalyze the search for sub-stitutes for scarce materials. Even com-panies that were meticulous about recycling scraps spent much of their time developing replacements.[46] Sometimes the task was simple. The Illinois Central Railroad used wood instead of aluminum shop patterns, cast iron instead of brass and copper, and asphalt and tar instead of rubber gas-

process, corporate and government re-searchers began to modify plans and invent new products. Every company poured much of its wartime profit into new laboratory facilities for the victory effort. Shure Brothers, an Evanston amplification equipment manufac-turer, designed throat and chest microphones that allowed hands-free operation on the bat-tlefield. Both Zenith and Western Electric played key roles in the development of radar and sonar, which were perhaps the two most important technological breakthroughs that aided the Allies. In addition, Western Electric helped develop the gun director, while Ze-nith's contributions included IFF ("Identi-fication Friend or Foe") equipment, homing receivers, and the radar height finder, which allowed ground observers to determine the altitude of incoming objects. Zenith also helped invent the "proximity fuze," which used

Chicago manufacturers produced nearly half of all military elec-tronic communication devices dur-ing the war. Below, the "Handie-Talkie" (popularly known as the walkie-talkie) produced by Galvin Corporation, which is now Motorola, Inc.

kets.[47] Other developments came less easily. Synthetic rubber remained almost as rare as the real thing during the war. Standard Oil and Diamond Wire & Cable Co., among others, worked on toluene and thiakol, the two leading substitutes.[48] Other scientists sought to create new metals. Several companies worked product applications of Monel, known for its corrosion resistance, into new product forms, while the Oscar Hedstrom Company announced with great fanfare the first public displays of "OH38," its new aluminum alloy.[49]

New products from wood and plastic also held promise. Mills Industries, a leading manufacturer of jukeboxes, the DeKalb piano works of the Wurlitzer Companies, and Naperville-based Kroehler Furniture Company all became involved in developing high-strength lightweight plywood for use as a substitute for metal aircraft skins. Wurlitzer actually built a number of wooden drone planes used for target practice. The Santay Corporation, which had made plastic auto dashboard parts and accessories such as steering-wheel spinners and stick-on ashtrays, developed radio equipment panels and knobs, windshields for airplanes, and similar substitutions of plastic for other materials. Meanwhile, Western Electric developed Lignin, a wood-fiber-based plastic for use as insulation inside of equipment.[50]

No industry involved as much direct contact between the soldier in the battlefield and the one in the lab coat as pharmaceuticals. Many decades had passed since armies routinely lost more of their fighting forces to disease than to battlefield trauma. Immunization and improved sanitation had eliminated the most serious hazards created by close physical contact. But World War II posed several new problems. One was the need to find substitutes for compounds that were no longer available from overseas. The G. D. Searle Company faced that problem when the war cut off supplies of belladonna from Italy, which was used to make atropine, an antispasmodic muscle relaxant. The company's scientists came up with a substitute.[51]

Military doctors were well aware of the hazards posed by malaria, a problem encountered by fighting a large-scale war in a tropical zone. Although quinine was effective against this jungle fever, difficulties in carrying supplies of it from South America through a war zone, plus the enormous size of the army to be treated, rendered the usual manufacturing procedures inadequate. The only answer lay in compressing development time, and Abbott Laboratories of North Chicago joined pharmaceutical manufacturers everywhere in giving uncommon diseases priority over domestic needs. Scientists at Abbott, in cooperation with Harvard University researchers, were still testing over two thousand antimalarial compounds on V-J Day.[52]

The war also forced medicine manufacturers to search for new ways to mass-produce known substances with a military value. One of the most curious ventures involved the find-

A selection of pharmaceuticals made by Abbott Laboratories during the war.

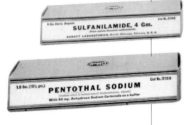

ing that serum albumin, a blood plasma extraction, helped limit blood loss from wounds. In June 1943 the government turned to Armour & Company; its decades of meat-packing experience had included experimentation with beef blood, which shares many characteristics with human blood. After it developed its techniques in its Chicago labs, Armour built a plant in Texas to extract the serum albumin from human blood.[53]

Only a small group of people knew about another research project that was underway on the South Side. Like many others, this, too, was directed and funded by the federal government. Its object was to make the first practical test of Albert Einstein's theory that it was possible to attain atomic fission, which would, in turn, release energy. It was widely known that German scientists had already conducted some preliminary experiments in the field, and federal officials realized the military potential of atomic fission. They instituted an emergency research project, with access to unlimited funds and resources, to build a bomb before the Germans did.

Although the work originated on the East Coast, the main research site chosen was an anonymous metallurgic laboratory established safely inland at the University of Chicago. Here, an elite group of forty physicists under the direction of Enrico Fermi began working under top-secret conditions during the early months of 1942. While they were headquartered in Eckhardt Hall, the focus of their attention was an unused squash court under the west stands of Stagg Field, the old stadium left virtually unused after the demise of intercollegiate football at the university.[54]

On December 2, 1942, the scientists were ready to see whether they could create a self-sustaining atomic reaction. They experimented all morning, studying the results. After lunch, Fermi decided to take the experiment

Below, artist Gary Sheehan's depiction of the first self-sustaining nuclear chain-reaction. Scientist Enrico Fermi (left) conducted the experiment that paved the way for the development of the atomic bomb.

to completion. Results proved that Einstein's theory was correct; the atomic reaction became self-sustaining. Although everything had gone exactly as Fermi had planned, the witnesses were awestruck. For better or for worse, the world had reached a turning point between 3:25 and 3:53 P.M. on a chilly Wednesday afternoon in the 5600 block of South Ellis Avenue.[55]

The Chicago group did not invent the atomic bomb. They only affirmed the theory that supported the design and construction of the device. Implementation, which was carried out elsewhere, took another thirty-three months. Chicagoans knew nothing of what had happened in their midst until after fire rained from the skies over Hiroshima and Nagasaki.

Top, worker security badge. Above, a decal announcing that Harrison High School students raised enough money to buy a P-51 Mustang fighter for the army.

Making It Work

It took much more than the talent of a handful of scientists to produce the complex variety of war goods that flowed from Chicago. Engineering know-how was useless without an army of skilled workers to make the detailed drawings, create the tools, run the machines, and pack and ship the goods. In turn, putting that labor in place was an equally complicated task: How do you find the workers? And how do you teach them the skills necessary to carry out their jobs? Creating a massive domestic army of workers involved recruiting them and then training them. The result was the largest and most intense technical education effort in America's as well as Chicago's history. All of the city, in effect, became an around-the-clock training ground.

The cornerstone of this training effort was the Chicago public school system. Students constructed thousands of model airplanes, which the navy used to teach aircraft identification to recruits. Students learned the use of tools and the principles of aeronautics as well. The normal curriculum for boys shifted emphasis to technical subjects, either in pre-induction courses such as radio and aviation shop or in skills that would prepare them for defense jobs after graduation. Metal shops upgraded their offerings to take into account new alloys, modern inspection procedures, and use of the latest precision tools and instruments—adjustments that reflected the more complex weaponry and communications equipment pouring from local factories. The war even altered the shop projects used to hone skills; traditional planting boxes and shoe scrapers gave way to equipment needed by hospitals and the Red Cross.[56]

Like Chicago industry, the school system shifted to an around-the-clock, seven-days-a-week production schedule. Building on a tradition of adult education that reached back nearly a century, it enlarged and modified a depression-era vocational program initiated in 1936. By May 1, 1942, approximately fifty thousand war workers had participated in classes that began after the final afternoon bell. Students learned radio, radar, shipbuilding, and basic machinist skills.[57]

The defense industry itself provided the second largest amount of employee training. Although costly, the numerous in-plant programs allowed employers to train a worker for a specific job in a minimum amount of time. Larger firms, such as Western Electric and International Harvester, had had the resources to do this for years. Others, like Stewart-Warner, which shifted entirely to war production, regarded themselves as schools and had nearly every employee involved in some type of training to ease into the retooling process. Plants that opened well into the war had to do the greatest amount of training, because so many of the most skilled workers were already at work in jobs, and government labor policies discouraged changing employers. In May 1942 Douglas and the Illinois State Board of Vocational Education had to open a special Aircraft School at 5001 West Madison Street to train the thousands of machinists and sheet metal workers it needed to start production.[58]

Programs established by area universities also helped to train workers. The University of Chicago offered classes in optical skills, meteorology, and defense industry office administration. Rosary College offered similar courses on a secretarial level. DePaul, Loyola, and Northwestern all offered training courses for women.[59] The Illinois Institute of Technology (IIT), created in 1940 by the merger of the Armour and Lewis Institutes of Technology, established the nation's first programs to teach advanced technical skills to women with some college background. The first class of 130 women ended their twelve-week program of classes in mathematics, engineering, and design in May 1942. By the time the program finally ended in August 1944, 1,089 women were certified. IIT also offered separate drafting courses as well as special courses for the military, in addition to its regular engineering offerings. By August 1944, a total of 48,689 students had enrolled in its various war programs.[60]

As the months of war passed, Chicago worked itself through phases in the creation of an industrial work force. The early months of the war actually saw a labor surplus. The unemployed, who still numbered near eighty thousand in June 1942, were among the first to take advantage of vocational training. When that pool was absorbed into the work force, the labor market began to expand to include groups that had not yet begun to share the wartime prosperity.

For the handicapped, the war became an opportunity to demonstrate their skills. The deaf had no problem working around noisy machinery, while the blind used their tactile powers to work with delicate equipment. One pharmaceutical firm in particular, George Barr & Co., gained wide publicity for its high productivity and low absentee rate from a work force that was almost exclusively handicapped. "A lot of prejudices and fixed ideas about handicapped people are being dropped overboard for the duration," said Frances Karlsteen of the Chicago Public Schools. "Actually, it is not what is gone that counts, but what is left."[61] Another group that was traditionally underutilized, little people, then called "midgets," found new employment opportunities at Douglas Aircraft, where they could maneuver power tools in places that were too small for workers of average size.[62]

From late 1942 through the end of the conflict, Chicago employers used every means possible to enlarge the work force. Thousands

of older workers came out of retirement. Douglas boasted that it had a sixty-eight-year-old sheet metal worker on its payroll. "Grandpa may not be what he used to be, but some of the jobs may be easier than he used to do," noted the *Tribune*.[63] Schoolteachers and high school students were encouraged to spend their summers working either in defense plants or on farms. The Illinois Central Railroad trained six hundred sixteen- and seventeen-year-old youths to replace brakemen, switchmen, and firemen.[64] The population of West Madison Street transients fell by 50 percent.[65] Even military personnel on furlough were allowed to hold part-time jobs in defense industries.

Above, workers with physical disabilities found more jobs available to them during the war. These workers are sewing a star on an Army-Navy E-Award flag at Belmont Radio Corporation.

Mildred Moore
The reason I enlisted—
I couldn't get a job. [My sister and I had] gone to [a] plant, and they weren't hiring blacks at that time. . . . They didn't say "blacks," but they said they didn't have any openings. . . . Yet . . . there was a whole line of whites standing in line waiting to go in. . . . And as we came out and we were coming down the line, [we got] catcalls and stuff like that. . . . I enlisted [in the WAC] because I couldn't get a job.

Many African-American workers found better employment opportunities during the war. A woman reconditions used spark plugs at the Buick Motors Division plant in Melrose Park, 1942.

The demand for labor reached beyond Chicago's borders. Railroad companies, which for decades had employed Mexican-American workers on track repair crews, now reached into Mexico itself to recruit over fifteen thousand immigrants over a two-year period late in the war. The steel industry, another traditional employer of Mexican-Americans, hired hundreds more. Most arrived with work permits that allowed them to stay only a few months at a time, but the city's small Mexican-American community gained seventy-five hundred permanent residents.[66]

The war also provided new opportunities for African-Americans, sixty-five thousand of whom moved from the South to Chicago. In 1940, the 15,694 black workers in Cook and DuPage counties made up only 2.8 percent of the work force. Only a few companies, such as Western Electric and International Harvester, hired significant numbers of minorities. Five years later, minorities made up 13.8 percent of the work force. Thousands traded low-paid menial jobs for industrial work or some of the choice service sector jobs that had been vacated by whites. The Chicago Surface Lines, for instance, hired the first black conductors in October 1943. Hundreds of black women benefited from a CIO-Chicago Urban League placement program that put them in every type of industry.[67]

These gains did not happen without a struggle. In the months before Pearl Harbor, it was clear to black leaders that their community was excluded from the economic benefits of the defense build-up. With the power of publicity as their main weapon, a group led by Chicagoan A. Philip Randolph, head of the locally based Brotherhood of Sleeping Car Porters, decided in early 1941 to organize a massive "March on Washington" to protest discrimination. Just as Randolph hoped, the Roosevelt administration realized the embarrassment such a protest might cause. On June 25, 1941, President Roosevelt issued Executive Order 8802, which forbade discrimination in any defense industries and government agencies. The order also established the Fair Employment Practices Committee (FEPC), whose first members included Chicagoans Earl Dickerson and Milton Webster. Although it could do no more than hold hearings and investigate wrongs, the FEPC helped open most of the larger defense plants to minorities.[68]

These gains, however, remained selective. Most jobs required few skills, and minorities who graduated from technical training programs still had a difficult time finding suitable employment. When they did, AFL craft unions admitted them only when ordered to do so. Black workers faced a particular obstacle in obtaining jobs during the later phases of the war because of the geography of industrial expansion. From the midpoint of the war until the end, the best new jobs were in the expanding aircraft industry, especially the larger Douglas, Buick, Studebaker, and Dodge-Chicago factories. But these companies were located on the periphery of the city, where public transit was sparse and slow, and few black workers owned cars. Racial segregation precluded living in adjacent neighborhoods.[69]

UNITED WE WIN

"Winning Democracy for the Negro is Winning the War for DEMOCRACY!"

50,000 NEGROES MARCH to the COLISEUM FRIDAY, JUNE 26, 1942 - 7 P.M.

In Mass Demonstration Against Discrimination and for Jobs

ADMISSION FREE

Auspices CHICAGO DIVISION MARCH ON WASHINGTON MOVEMENT

Left, government posters encouraged workers of different races to work together toward the common goal of defeating the Axis. The reality of employment in the city, however, was often different. Above, a poster announcing a march against employment discrimination. Shown is A. Philip Randolph, who organized the massive "March on Washington."

Right, companies aggressively recruited women for war work. Opposite, with many male baseball players in the service, women's softball leagues became popular.

Women at the Gates

Women constituted the largest category of newcomers to the work force. Some contributed indirectly to the defense effort by replacing not only men, but also other women who had taken factory jobs. The departure of women from jobs in domestic service and retail clerking to better-paying employment meant the substitution of less-experienced women for those jobs. Restaurant patrons complained when slower and less attentive help replaced their favorite waitresses.

Women contributed to the work force through assuming nontraditional jobs, which in turn freed up men for either military service or employment in a defense plant. A number of unusual occupations gave the press a field day describing the various ways women stepped outside of their usual domestic roles. Professional baseball attracted the most attention. Chewing gum magnate Philip K. Wrigley had seen the ranks of all professional ball teams, including the Chicago White Sox and his own Chicago Cubs, decimated by the draft. Fans often derided less-talented substitute players. In 1943 Wrigley and Branch Rickey, gambling that disgruntled fans would come out to see a game played with excellence by women, formed the All-American Girls Professional Baseball League. Each season featured 120 games among the ten midwestern teams, which were primarily located in medium-sized industrial cities.[70]

Some of the first job opportunities for women in the work force involved replacing men who had moved up from low-paid service occupations to more lucrative defense industry jobs. Female elevator operators became common months before Pearl Harbor. The *Daily News* described the "fondness for outside work" as one reason why women took jobs as garbage collectors. Many women also took advantage of the fact that because of modern mechanization, many of the new jobs required more skill than physical strength. The Illinois Central Railroad began hiring female train crews by 1943.[71] Women made even more progress in the rapidly expanding trucking business. By the end of 1942, Virginia MacLean worked for the Keeshin Motor Express Company, which claimed that she was the nation's first female long-haul trucker. Eventually, women drove mail trucks, streetcars, and taxis. In one highly publicized incident, the navy bused one hundred women to Ottumwa, Iowa, to drive a convoy of heavy construction trucks back to Chicago for repairs. Company operators were pleased. "These women are better drivers than the men were," noted the army officer in charge of the Sixth Service Command garage about his twenty-eight female truckers.[72]

Women also found employement in security and authority jobs. A North Clark Street bar hired a female bouncer. In June 1943, the Chicago Park District hired its first women lifeguards, a job requiring great strength and swimming skills. Three years earlier, the park district had begun hiring women as part-time "service guards," the traffic police assigned to school crossings. Northwestern University began admitting women to its police administration courses early in 1942.[73]

Lou Lunak

I was the only woman in [the tool and die] department; hundreds of men. There was one Afro-American guy there too, and [we] were sort of like tokens, I guess. . . . I worked on a milling machine. I had a 3/1000 [inch] tolerance [margin of error from production specifications] and some of the older guys that were on the bench where they assigned the jobs, they didn't want to give me their job, "Ugh, a girl couldn't do that!". . . . So finally this one guy had to me one of his jobs because I was the only one available. . . . When I got it done it came out 1/1000 tolerance. . . . He thought that was good, so he wanted me to do his jobs after that! . . . And they wanted to write me up in the company paper, and the men said "No, we don't want our wives to know a girl can do our work!"

Above, inspectors at Studebaker's Chicago Aviation Plant examine finished products before shipping. One of the lasting effects of the war was the increased emphasis on quality control in manufacturing.

The need to fill vacant job positions also brought women in unprecedented numbers into downtown offices. Although women had been working in offices since the late nineteenth century, men made up most of the ranks of downtown office employees until the war, when federal officials began to advise managers to train women to take over all jobs performed by men. In some large banks, for instance, the female portion of the work force grew from one-third in March 1941 to 55 percent a year later to over 60 percent in May 1943. According to one October 1943 survey, 53 percent of all office workers were female. A year later, their share stood at 70 percent.[74] During the summer of 1943, the Chicago Board of Trade allowed young women to serve as pages, the first time in its ninety-five-year history that women had been allowed on its trading floor.[75]

Besides freeing up other workers for defense jobs, women joined the check-in lines at plant gates in unprecedented numbers. Often the length of time a particular factory had been in business determined the extent of these opportunities. Recently formed corpora-

tions frequently suffered the largest losses to the military because their male workers were relatively young; women made up the bulk of the replacements. Older, heavy-industry plants continued to have a male work force. Despite the publicity surrounding their new jobs, female steel workers were relatively rare. The ALCOA rolling mill, however, employed many women because the automated rolling mills required little heavy lifting. Other fields, such as electronics, had employed large numbers of women long before the war.

How late in the war the company obtained large contracts also determined opportunities for women. Firms that expanded rapidly after 1943, when the draft quotas grew, had no choice but to hire women. As the war progressed, and the number of contracts for pharmaceuticals, dehydrated foods, and complex communications and navigation systems expanded, job opportunities for women widened proportionally. The press and company officials, however, could not help linking the new jobs to traditional housework skills. Smaller hands, "nimble fingers," and domestic sewing skills opened up opportunities in assembling small electronic parts and precision machine milling work.[76]

The entry of women into factory work forced the reconsideration of traditional policies and customs. Work near moving machinery made loose-fitting dresses, jewelry, and long hair dangerous. Companies encouraged women to wear "Jeepsuit" coveralls or coat/slacks combinations with low-heeled "Victory Industrial Shoes." Douglas Aircraft held employee fashion shows demonstrating how rayon-blend fabrics kept wrinkle-free "for several days at a time" and resisted perspiration stains.[77]

Women's work attire might never have become a matter of widespread discussion had it stayed within the walls of the factory. But many older companies either had no employee locker rooms or those segregated by gender, so many women commuted in their work clothes. This upset many traditionalists. One man spouted biblical quotations—"A woman shall not wear that which pertaineth unto a man"; another fumed, "Can a real he-man have any respect for a woman who parades in the streets in man's clothes?"[78] The issue reached a peak in January 1943, when police arrested a twenty-year-old war worker for violating the city ordinance that forbade "appearing in public in a state of nudity or in dress not belonging to his or her sex." The publicity surrounding her conviction persuaded the city council to alter the law by adding the provision "with intent to conceal his or her sex."[79]

The addition of women to the factory raised other issues, including the safety and well-being of women who were not used to rugged factory work. Many newspaper readers were doubtless shocked to learn that at the Elwood Arsenal more than half of the large work force that loaded TNT into 105-mm howitzer shells and bombs were women. Their tan coveralls were completely lacking any metal zippers or buttons that might cause a spark.[80] In his *Tribune* column, Dr. Irving Cutter worried that women who were both homemakers and defense workers would exhaust themselves and thus risk contracting and spreading tuberculosis. Ironically, though, the press frequently dismissed female workers' requests for shorter hours and work furloughs as frivolous.[81]

Working For Victory

The large defense factory was a new world for workers. Many were impersonal cities within a city, where management tread the thin line between a heavy-handed control over the

Above, a woman's navy blue coverall outfit. Due to safety considerations, women in factories were encouraged to wear simple work clothing, which many considered too "masculine." Left, a woman wears safety goggles, gloves, and protective clothing as she cuts metal at a U.S. Steel plant in Gary, Indiana.

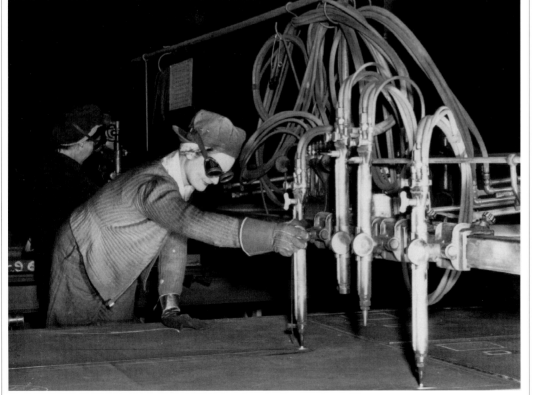

Right, workers assemble film projectors for the navy at National Mineral Co., now Helene Curtis Industries, Inc.

work force and the creation of a happy family. The war emergency justified strict controls. Plant security was tight, and employee identification badges and widespread fingerprinting appeared for the first time during the war. "No alien may enter the plant and to enter with a camera requires almost everything but an act of Congress," the Western Electric *Microphone* reminded its readers. In the wake of Pearl Harbor, Western Electric doubled its police force, checked every inbound freight car, put heavy screens on windows facing streets, and increased outdoor lighting.[82] Worner Products Corporation offered "Worner's Anti-sabotage Equipment . . . individually engineered to protect your plant against intruders both day and night. Electric-eye coverage available in ranges of 250 to 500 feet."[83]

During the early part of the war, many plants also encouraged their workers to listen in to the conversations of fellow employees and report anything suspicious. Defense contractors were also on the alert against sabotage in the form of rumors. Douglas Aircraft, for example, set up a special column in its house organ, *Douglas-Chicago Airview News*, to squelch rumors that the company was making excess profits, that African-Americans were no longer being hired, and that the plant would be phased out soon after the war.[84]

Companies quickly initiated psychological campaigns to mold the new work force into an ideal industrial army. There were special awards for perfect attendance and mock trials for chronic absentees and those guilty of tardiness. Company newsletters listed the names of those calling in sick, in part to encourage fellow employees to inform on them. One defense contractor, Pioneer Gen-E Co., went as far as to ask its workers, 60 percent of whom were women, to curb dating because, in the words of one of its safety advisors,

"Romance keeps people out late at night—sometimes too late and the next morning they don't feel like getting up for work."[85]

Cartoons, posters, lectures, and films stressed plant safety, especially in the wake of such disasters as the June 5, 1942, explosion at Elwood, which killed forty-eight workers.[86] The most important goal was increasing output using fewer workers and smaller amounts of materials. Inspectors repeatedly pored over everything produced in an effort to turn out a perfect product, and workers were constantly reminded that indifference on their part might result in someone—perhaps a loved one—being killed by a faulty piece of equipment. Shortages of raw materials resulted in a campaign against waste in any form. Sloganeering was apparent everywhere: "Scratch Those Scratches" advised posters at Douglas.[87]

Defense contractors also stressed the "reward," as well as the "punishment" side of the dual effort to maximize efficiency and output. They gave cash bonuses and recognition to employees who submitted useful ideas to the omnipresent suggestion box. Because most jobs had been broken down into component parts and much of the work had become monotonous machine-tending, managers realized that their most formidable enemy was not sabotage, but employee fatigue and lapses in morale. As a result, the larger the plant, the greater the emphasis on creating a tightly knit work community that functioned in the workplace much in the same manner that neighborhoods created a sense of caring unity. Company newspapers broke down the barriers of anonymity by publishing photographs and biographical trivia about employees. Companies also fostered employee clubs around such interests as gardening, music, roller skating, hunting, bowling, and other activities to encourage fraternizing outside of the workplace.[88]

Defense plant propaganda also urged workers to find alternatives to the one-person commute to work in the family auto. Defense workers were given priority in the purchase of bicycles. Although used primarily by those lucky enough to live close to their work, Swift and a few other companies put their salesmen on bicycles. Steel and rubber rationing had halted the rebirth of popular interest in cycling for leisure almost before it started. In March 1942 government regulations cut bicycle production by over half and limited it to men's and women's versions of a single lightweight "defense model." There were no gadgets, lights, or chrome trim, and no children's sizes.[89]

Another option was car pooling, which gained popularity midway through 1942. The *Daily News* claimed to be the first paper in the nation to print car-pool notices free of charge. A nationwide share-a-ride campaign and catchy slogans, such as "Who Rides Alone Rides With Hitler," helped as well. Some large companies like Western Electric had for decades taken advantage of their size to pro-

THE ONLY CLOCK TO WATCH — THE ONLY PAY DAY THAT COUNTS

mote shared rides. Douglas and other firms that arrived in the area later, however, had a double obstacle because they had a late start in assembling their work force. They had to lure workers from existing plants, and this often meant that employees' homes were scattered across a wide area. Their plants were also located so far out on the fringe that there was very little adjacent housing. One Douglas employee, for example, spent four hours and ten minutes commuting a total of eighty-six miles each day by streetcar and car pool. Nonetheless, the aircraft maker joined other companies in either denying parking privileges to solo drivers or making such employees park in the most distant lot.[90]

A 1942 editorial cartoon by Gary Orr for the *Chicago Tribune* emphasizes workers' importance in winning the war.

Workers and management took great pride in receiving the Army-Navy E-Award. Below, the Midwest Forging and Manufacturing Company hoists an E-Award flag. Opposite, employees of companies winning the award received E-pins like this one.

Factory efforts at boosting morale included adaptations of one major element in the WPB procurement plan—what might be called "the big goal." Like bond and scrap drives, it was never enough to exhort Americans to do more or work harder. Officials provided incentive by setting measurable goals, either in speed or in total quantity of output. For instance, when Douglas Aircraft created its gigantic Chicago plant, it was not content merely to "do its best" to produce its first C-54 by mid-summer 1943. It used every opportunity to repeat the slogan "Fly By July," which appeared all over plant walls, in the company newsletter, in the contest to choose a beauty queen ("Miss Fly By July"), and in frequent pep talks to employees. Douglas achieved its goal when the C-54 Skymaster *Chicago* took off on July 30, 1943.

Military procurement offices established another "big goal" incentive through the recognition of plants whose performance was almost perfect, an echo of the V-Home award, which rewarded perfection in individual households. During the first part of the war, the army and navy had individually issued awards to outstanding suppliers, but in July 1942 the programs were combined into the Army-Navy E-Awards, which recognized company excellence. Corporations whose employees demonstrated outstanding attendance and safety records, maintained the most harmonious labor-management relations, and exceeded production goals could be nominated by the branch of the military to which they supplied most of their production. Further review by officials in Washington led to the award.[91]

Plants took great pride in the award. Notification came in a telegram, which was followed a few days later by officers who set up the standardized ceremony. No one complained that programs of military pomp, congratulatory speeches, and martial music were virtually identical to those staged at other companies. For years afterwards, recipients remained proud that they received a brightly colored banner and got to fly a distinctive

Army-Navy "E-Flag" under the American flag on the front flagpole. Only about 5 percent of the nation's eighty-five thousand defense suppliers earned the award. About 10 percent of the winners were in Illinois, 233 of them in the city of Chicago. The suburbs boasted seventy-four winners.[92]

Despite the patriotic contribution of sharply increased hours with no overtime pay, workers complained remarkably little. Organized labor contributed to the stability of the situation after Pearl Harbor by participating in company personnel committees to iron out disagreements and pledging not to strike.[93] This contrasted sharply with the tumult of the late 1930s, when violent walkouts accompanied efforts to regain wages and jobs lost during the depression. Statewide, there were fewer strikes during the war than in the single year 1941. The

Lynn Abbie
We had the car pool and it would have been almost impossible any other way. They had a very elaborate and very solid setup, and you would get priority rationing cards.
. . . The carpooler would like [to offer to drive other workers]. Not only did he get paid from each person who was riding with him, but he had this wonderful gas supply because he was carpooling.
I can remember that Douglas Aircraft had one department that was just carpooling! . . . You got out there to be hired; they'd see to it that the next day you'd have somebody driving you in.
. . . I often think that [carpooling] really conserved and saved a lot. It was economically sound in every way in terms of time, in terms of fuel; cost-effective, too.

Women examine a carpooling map showing the residences of workers at the Buick plant in Melrose Park, 1942.

President Roosevelt examines a special globe manufactured by the Weber Costello Co. of Chicago Heights. Copies of the globe were sent to the U.S. War Department, Winston Churchill, and Joseph Stalin to ensure good communication about war developments.

labor stoppages that did take place were unauthorized walkouts that involved relatively few workers, although the press expressed concern that it took relatively few workers to stop production of complex weapons. Issues troubling workers included the failure of the companies to grant a wash-up time at the end of a work period or the disciplining of a fellow worker. Rather than trying to correct a massive injustice, walkouts served to let management know that workers had feelings and were more than automatons.[94]

The most famous walkout of the war, in fact, involved a company, rather than a union, going on strike. Sewell L. Avery, the head of Montgomery Ward & Company, refused to comply with the regulations of the War Labor Board, the federal agency established to control labor-management regulations. Avery contended that the catalog house was not technically an industry and therefore could manage its own affairs. The Roosevelt administration argued that not only did mail-order companies see themselves as an industry, but that Ward's subsidiary producers functioned as a defense contractors. In the spring of 1944, Roosevelt issued an executive order placing the firm under government control. U.S. Army personnel seized the building, and two soldiers carried the cantankerous Avery out of his office, depositing him on the street.

The Ward incident was more symbolic than substantive. The company was not a major defense supplier, but the newspapers and newsreels gave top billing to the case. The conservative press and the business community rallied to Avery's cause, implying that Roosevelt was assuming dictatorial powers that might lead to a military seizure of all rights as well as property. Labor groups, on the other hand, saw it as case where a vehemently antiunion crusader had been forced to put patriotic production before profit. Companies, they argued, forced adherence to government rules only when it was profitable. Pundits pointed out that "S. L. Avery" spelled "slavery." Ultimately, the federal government won a prolonged court battle over its authority to enforce War Labor Board decrees.[95]

✪   ✪   ✪   ✪   ✪   ✪

The story of industrial Chicago during World War II is remarkable. A demoralized local economy seized the opportunity to remake itself into the country's second largest arsenal, maker of the most sophisticated weapons America possessed. The story was a unique part of the city's wartime experience, yet it also reflects some of the common factors that shaped the home and the neighborhood experience. Decades of technological and industrial evolution occurred in a few short years. The slow industrial start-up in 1941–42 and gradual shutdown during 1945 meant that most of this story took place in only thirty months. The compression of time was unlike anything seen in the city's history, even the rebuilding after the Great Fire of 1871.

Industrial history is also the story of things, and, like households, factories found that they had to "do more with less." The result was innovation. Just as the consumers experimented with substitutes, so, too, did industrialists turn to the laboratory and the suggestion box because of scarce materials or machinery. Although World War II is justifiably remembered for its battlefield and shipboard heroism, it was also a research experience, a scientific victory, and a technological boom of enormous proportions. This helped make it an educational miracle as well. Just as civilian defense could be characterized as an experiment in mass learning, the massive technical training effort to produce an industrial army was unlike anything Chicago or the nation had encountered before or since.

The war uprooted all aspects of life. Not only did it take the young man or woman from down the block to faraway lands, but it also plucked Chicagoans from their accustomed work worlds, putting new tools in their hands and new goals in their minds. The big defense plant was an eerie experience for

many, in part because the requirements of security and the urgency of the work allowed the factory to intrude into workers' private lives to an unprecedented degree. Management encouraged workers to inform on each other. Leisure hours were organized by a recreation department. Overtime robbed the family of its time together. British author George Orwell did not complete *1984* until 1949, but he sensed the dehumanizing aspects of a homefront organized on a massive scale.

Chicago artist Samuel Greenburg submitted this poster to a competition sponsored by The Art Institute of Chicago.

The face of the city was transformed by the presence of service personnel. On any given day, tens of thousands of servicemen passed through Chicago's many rail terminals, such as Union Station (right).

The Crossroads City

During the war years, Chicagoans seemed constantly in motion. People on their way to work rubbed shoulders with passengers transferring between depots and throngs returning from bond rallies. The depression of the 1930s had forced an air of lassitude on the city and left its streets empty of shoppers and rush-hour workers. The railroads slashed schedules, and the Chicago police broke up curbside rallies lest they offer a forum for political radicals. But the war revitalized the public spaces of Chicago—its streets, sidewalks, parks, and institutions—with not only a new sense of prosperity, but also an atmosphere of urgency.

With this movement came intermingling and a return to the sense of the city as a crossroads. It was an exchange, an agglomeration of not only material, but of different peoples, neighborhoods, communities, ideas, attitudes, and loyalties. Chicago functioned as an interchange on two levels. One was purely local and involved how individuals got along with each other, how they defined the parameters of their neighborhoods, and what unified and divided them.

But Chicago also acted as a national and international crossroads, a function that had also been a central factor in the build-up of defense plants. Chicago's industrial base had been diversified for decades because of the ease with which shippers moved every type of raw material in and all varieties of finished goods out to American markets. The factories, in turn, attracted workers from across the country and around the world. The same railroads that carried grain, cement, and livestock also carried passengers, making Chicago the place where Americans changed trains. In wartime, however, this human interchange function took on new meaning and gave the city an opportunity to present an image to America that, for a time at least, pushed aside that of Al Capone.

Victory Plaza and the Big Event

Wartime activities in the home and the neighborhood took place in familiar settings. Events touched individual families and neighbors, who were often also friends. Public demonstrations and parades took place in streets and parks on familiar turf. The wartime workplace, on the other hand, frequently drew people away from the familiar places and faces. Workers in large defense plants were part of an anonymous crowd, despite the efforts by corporations to generate a sense of community through plant newspapers and social activities. The security gate represented an intermingling of workers from many neighborhoods, but the ultimate crossroads of Chicago was the Loop and its environs. Throughout the war, the city's heart was also the focus of the most public—and most anonymous—crowd participation in the homefront effort.

The significance of the Loop grew out of the manner in which the federal and local governments sustained morale. No one knew how long "the duration" would actually be; some estimates held that it might take as long as a decade to defeat two major enemies. Such a prolonged conflict required a series of specific goals that were like mileposts along a road.

Pin worn by USO hostesses, who were called "Victory Belles."

97

The Loop was the focal point for many patriotic activities, such as the "Air WAC" recruitment corner at State and Madison, and for parades, such as those on Michigan Avenue.

Scrap drives were organized in this manner: specific amounts were to be collected by specific dates. The most important use of this technique, however, was in the govenrment's eight major bond drives.

Within weeks of the sinking of the USS *Chicago* on January 30, 1943, off Guadalcanal, the *Daily News* had contacted the navy and established the target of $40 million, to be collected only within the borders of Chicago, to finance its replacement. Money poured in from such groups as the B'nai B'rith, the Pan-Hellenic Federation, and Lithuanian groups commemorating the twenty-fifth anniversary of the Red Army. Chicago's public schools authorized the voluntary collection of a penny from each student. Tens of thousands of Chicagoans made special bond purchases, most of them in the twenty-five-dollar denomination. The goal was reached in only forty days.[1]

Building morale also involved a series of special events, crowd-pleasing affairs in which individuals witnessed demonstrations, entertainment, and speech-making that impressed upon people the importance of working hard or buying bonds "until it hurts." These great gatherings sometimes opened campaigns toward specific goals. The size of the throng added to the impression of moral certitude. Both the United States and its enemies had utilized this technique for years.[2]

Special events also substituted for holiday celebrations, which fell victim to wartime shortages and restrictions. Fourth of July celebrations, for example, lacked fireworks because explosives were needed on the battlefront, and because fewer war workers would lose their fingers trying to shoot them off. Because Independence Day was designated as a regular workday, the crowds were thinned anyway.[3]

One of the first special patriotic spaces created was Congress Street Plaza, the widened intersection at Michigan Avenue. Its functions were primarily related to military recruiting, rather than fund-raising or general patriotic purposes. As part of the recruiting drives of the summer of 1942, city workers erected a large replica of the bow of a battleship, complete

with anchors and three large cannons. Atop the structure stood a large circular dial that registered naval recruitment. Here Chicago commemorated the six-month anniversary of Pearl Harbor with one of the first big ceremonies of the war.[4] As the war continued, this elaborately contrived space was also used to commemorate Memorial Day and to honor soldiers who were killed.[5]

The concentration of economic activities in or near the Loop provided the stage for a variety of patriotic activities. The Loop contained Chicago's major theaters, which included a number of shows with military themes. *This is the Army, Mr. Jones*, the Irving Berlin production featuring three hundred actual soldiers, was a smash hit both as a live stage show at the Civic Opera House and later as a motion picture at the Chicago Theatre. Smaller shows such as *The Army Play by Play* and *War Communicade*, both with all-soldier casts, added to the military atmosphere of downtown, as did the many war-related movie titles on theater marquees.[6]

The railroad stations downtown were decorated with flags and banners. Two giant banners virtually covered opposite walls of the concourse building of Union Station. One read, "For Us—Bonds"; the one opposite read, "For Them—Bombs." Overhead were hundreds of small model airplanes suspended from the ceiling. Volunteers operated a busy canteen for service personnel, who made up a substantial portion of the travelers who filled both the concourse and waiting room buildings. Every depot was jammed, and in at least one instance, a panic broke out among passengers vying for the last remaining seats on a holiday train.[7]

Many depot arrivals were commuters and shoppers on their way to State Street. The world's busiest shopping thoroughfare served many purposes. Its department stores not only

dominated local retailing through their size and the variety of items they offered, but they were also the scene of many war-related events. In 1942, Marshall Field & Co. opened its Victory Center, which provided a popular education in gardening, food conservation and cooking, wartime fashions, and other war-related topics. Carson Pirie Scott & Co., Goldblatt's, the Boston Store, and the Fair also drew crowds to special events. Most store windows contained messages urging Chicagoans to buy bonds or give blood.[8]

The concourse of Chicago's Union Station boasted the "world's largest patriotic display." The Society of Typographic Artists suspended model airplanes from the ceiling and painted large murals at each end of the concourse.

Peter Johnsen
Union Station was the O'Hare Airport of its period. It was always packed, twenty-four hours a day.... It was unbelievably jammed with people and probably half or two-thirds were service people passing through.... We went to Iowa several times [during the war], but it was torture.... It took about fourteen hours to get there.... What took so long was that passenger trains had the lowest priority. See, everything was prioritized. Troop trains and freight trains were at the top of the list.... I can remember with the warm weather, with the windows open, maybe if it was a still night, and maybe a half mile away the trains, endless, with the freight trains rumbling. It was a constant. Anyways, it took forever to get to Iowa because you were constantly being sidetracked.... It wasn't fun.

Downtown Chicago became one of the military's most effective forums for the explanation of the war to the general public. Each summer, the *Tribune* held a month-long War Products Display, at which Chicago manufacturers showed off the tangible results of their nonclassified war contracts. Visitors could climb aboard tanks, help load mock shells, or see what it was like to operate a gunnery trainer. Meanwhile, State Street's sidewalks were lined with similar weapon displays during bond drives in what was virtually an outdoor military museum. In August 1943, the display at State and Madison streets included an eighty-one-foot, two-man submarine captured from the Japanese.[9]

Soldier Field, Burnham Park, and State Street itself were the scene of large displays of Allied and enemy equipment and demonstrations in which personnel staged sham battles and demonstrated the use of different equipment.[10] One "gas attack" completely enshrouded the busy street at high noon in dense black smoke.[11] "That Great Street" also had "Victory Corner" at Van Buren Street, where celebrities performed to noontime crowds to sell bonds.[12] Even the Chicago River was pressed into service when, in June 1943, the Army Corps of Engineers celebrated their 168th anniversary by constructing a pontoon bridge across it at State Street in fifty-five minutes.[13]

Parades on Michigan Avenue and State Street were, of course, a constant feature of the patriotic public place. Throngs lined the street to kick off bond and scrap drives and to greet heroes. The Hollywood Victory Caravan, held at the Chicago Stadium on May 6, 1942, to raise funds for army and navy relief, started with a big procession down Michigan Avenue.[14] One of the largest processions was held in honor of Gen. Douglas MacArthur on the anniversary of his entrance into West Point; he, of course, was "at work" in Australia.[15]

The centrality of the Loop and State Street were best symbolized by what happened as Chicago learned of the much-expected D-Day invasion of Normandy on June 6, 1944. All across the city, there were short prayer services and moments of silence in factories. Many Chicagoans rushed to Red Cross blood donation centers, as well as to churches and synagogues. Despite a driving rain, hundreds attended a 5:30 P.M. prayer service that Mayor Kelly hastily arranged. The logical place: State and Madison.[16]

Some activities did not fit downtown. Because it operated in water, the navy was somewhat less visible in the Loop itself, except for its recruiting activities at Congress Street Square. Nearby Navy Pier, however, was a perfect site for morale-building public events. Its "Pacific Theater" show of November 1944 featured a hospital ship, a Hellcat equipped for jet-assisted take-offs, rockets, radio receivers, and landing craft, the latter also used by the Marine Corps to stage mock invasions of the Foster Avenue Beach.[17]

The Loop also played an important role in providing a spectacular opening for most of the major bond drives and linking them to the neighborhood and factory selling efforts. The first was somewhat less focused than its successors, kicking off with the appearance of actor-comedian Jimmy Durante at the Ashland

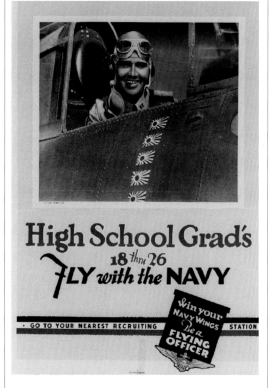

Opposite, a USO club at Union Station. Left, "Butch" O'Hare poses in his fighter plane for the navy. Above, recruitment posters were common sights in public places. Program for the "Hollywood Victory Caravan," a benefit at the Chicago Stadium that featured many Hollywood film stars.

Chicagoans participated in many fund-raising and patriotic events downtown. Above, almost 790,000 people attended this army war show at Soldier Field in 1942. Opposite, Norman Rockwell's cover for the *Saturday Evening Post* captures the holiday bustle at North Western Station.

Auditorium. By contrast, the second drive, which began on April 12, 1943, set the pace for the rest of the war. The site of many of these rallies was "Victory Plaza," which was nothing more than the west face of City Hall festooned with huge banners overlooking LaSalle Street. Fifteen-foot-wide golden eagles—their wings forming a "V"—topped pylons that reached the fifth floor, where the mayor's office was located. In the middle stood a two-story-tall portrait of President Roosevelt, no doubt a disturbing visage to the conservative bankers who passed by it every day.[18]

Although most bonds were sold door-to-door, in stores, and in the workplace, downtown

bond drives featured more Hollywood entertainment, more giant signs monitoring progress toward the goal, and more events such as "Sacrifice Day," in which citizens were asked to give up something in order to buy a bond. Norman Rockwell's famous *Four Freedoms* paintings made an appearance at Carson Pirie Scott as part of the fourth bond drive.[19]

Soldier Field was another perfect patriotic arena. Army war shows, bond rallies, and other gatherings of cheering crowds were held here, but as the war progressed, one annual event there reflected the growing sense of fear that underlay the public optimism: the candlelight services sponsored each summer by the Roman Catholic Archdiocese. Emotional crowds of as many as 150,000 recited prayers, heard sermons, and witnessed somber processions that mixed military equipment, the parents of living and dead service personnel, and religious leaders.[20] These events, covered in sober reports by national newsreel companies, revealed the difficulty of sustaining optimism through four years.

As the war dragged on, even the special events began to lose their luster. Challenged ad writers at Marshall Field's began contriving gimmicks, such as the "Wanna Jeep Cheap?" contest, in which the purchaser of a fifty-dollar bond received an entry blank on which they explained, in a hundred words or less, "What I'll do with my Jeep." The winner drove one home.[21] Perhaps the most telling development in maintaining morale came in early 1944 when Mayor Kelly told a reporter, "We must do something to get people back to the Pearl Harbor spirit." Weariness and a false sense of impending victory had produced what Kelly called "a slump that is affecting the war effort all along the line, including bond sales and plasma donations as well as manpower." Even his appointment of a Committee for Patriotic Action could do little to revive war morale.[22]

Crossroads Within a Crossroads

Despite Mayor Kelly's efforts to decentralize the direction of day-to-day activities, the Loop remained their central focus. It was the place from which orders for air raid drills and scrap drives originated. It was also home to the news media, to which Chicagoans turned for information that might provide a clue to the fate of a loved one or neighbor in the service. The major newspapers not only had their own battlefield correspondents, but also functioned as mass educators. Readers who had never ventured outside of the city limits could now recite a list of Pacific atolls or cities located along the Rhine. Radio stations, which were also clustered downtown and on North Michigan Avenue, devoted much air time to war news, victory garden hints, and interviews with military personnel.[23]

Even more important was downtown Chicago's function as a national crossroads. Chicago was America's rail transportation hub. This role, which dated back to the mid-1850s, became even more pronounced during World War II because rationing limited the use of private automobiles, and because the military took control of much of the nation's airline equipment. America rode the train.

Chicago's inland location and transportation advantages played a key role in several unexpected developments. One was the location of prisoner-of-war camps at Fort Sheridan, Techny, and other places in the metropolitan area. The central inland location of the city made it a convenient spot from which they could be moved to where their labor was needed.[24]

In addition, the fear of enemy bombing, along with the proliferation of the government bureaucracy during the war, prompted the Roosevelt administration to create the Office of Decentralization Service to move nonmilitary agencies out of Washington. The surplus of vacant Loop office space made Chicago especially attractive, and within days of the attack on Pearl Harbor, *Daily News* headlines announced "Big Migration: U.S. Offices Coming West."[25] The first arrivals came in April 1942, when the Railroad Retirement Board moved 1,761 workers to 844 North Rush Street. Within six months, the Alien Assets Administration, Office of Indian Affairs, U.S. Maritime Commission, and Federal Bureau of Debt had moved their central offices to the city. The Social Security Board, Federal Housing Administration, War Labor Board, Office of Defense Transportation, Fair Employment Practices Commission, War Production Board, Office of Civilian Defense, Office of Price Administration, Office of Emergency Management, Treasury Department, and Federal Reserve decentralized much of their operations to major regional offices in the city. Most U.S. savings bonds were processed in Chicago.[26]

Altogether, "Little Washington," as the *Tribune* called it, saw over seventy-five hundred workers arrive over a period of eighteen months.

Sandee Grossman
From Fort Sheridan and Great Lakes, [soldiers came] in on the north line of the [Chicago and] North Western [Railroad], and they'd have ten and twelve and fifteen coaches. You can get ninety people on those coaches. . . . And at that time there was . . . a center stairway [in the station] that was about as wide as this room. And they'd come in and down—you'd see a sea of whatever color it was coming in at that time.

When my brothers and I used to stand and watch the freights go out at Proviso [Railroad] Yards, 125 cars, 150, maybe 200 being pulled by three or four good old large, smoke-stacked, puffers. You'd wait half an hour for them to pass by. Different war goods, some of the huge equipment that was made, [was] strapped on [the trains]. And there were no photographs taken, there was nothing. And they would pass by. There was a lot during the night that went too.

Top, the army took over a number of vacant buildings in the Central Manufacturing District. Middle, Bartlett Gymnasium at the University of Chicago was turned into temporary quarters for the military trainees on campus. Right, University of Chicago professors taught many technical courses to military trainees.

Operations were scattered in small offices at first, but federal decentralization officials quickly realized the efficiency of consolidating offices into three principal sites. One was the building at Jackson Boulevard and Franklin Street, which had stood empty since the Chicago & North Western Railroad moved its headquarters in 1929. The two others symbolized the prosperous 1920s: the Civic Opera Building and the Merchandise Mart, the world's largest office building. Noting that by December 1943 vacant office space downtown had fallen by 25 percent, Business Week quipped, "Many a white elephant is finally paying off."[27]

Because the Chicago area played such an essential role in military training, the military presence in the central area was ubiquitous. This critical function was organized in a manner that matched the economic geography of the region. At the periphery of the region stood the two basic training facilities, which required the most space. Here, the region's history shaped wartime events. Chicago's central rail hub location had long made it efficient for that purpose because it reduced travel time from any part of the nation. But the war added the element of security from attack as well. The oldest facility was Fort Sheridan, founded twenty-seven miles north of the city in the aftermath of the 1886 Haymarket Affair. Nearly closed during the depression, it was revived in 1938 and became one of the largest induction reception centers, processing 417,000 recruits during the war.[28]

Meanwhile, Great Lakes Naval Training Center, located forty-two miles north of Chicago, underwent a $75 million expansion, making it the navy's largest single reception and training center. At any one time, its on-base personnel numbered between fifty and seventy thousand. By the war's end, over one million sailors—one out of every three who served during World War II—passed through its gates.[29]

In 1940 the navy opened the third Chicago-area training center with the purchase of the eleven-year-old Curtiss-Wright Airport in Glenview, twenty miles northwest of the Loop. Described initially as a "sleepy post [with] class-es of a dozen prospective naval air cadets," it underwent a dramatic $12.5 million transfor-mation. By March 1943 it had become the largest of the navy's primary air training units, with one thousand aviation cadets turned out every three months.[30]

Left, an army recruit is outfitted at Fort Sheridan. Below, sailors at Great Lakes Naval Training Center. About one third of all naval recruits were trained at the center.

Above, naval cadet officers march in front of the Illinois National Guard Armory at Chicago Avenue and the lakefront. Opposite above, soldiers cross Michigan Avenue on a temporary bridge to get to the Stevens Hotel, which the army used for a radio technicians' school in 1942. Opposite below, army personnel enjoy some good times rollerskating at Riverview Park.

Glenview was also the home base for one of the war's most unusual experiments. The threat to the American coasts and the highly unpredictable ocean weather conditions made the more placid Great Lakes an attractive alternative for aircraft carrier pilot training. The big obstacle was the shortage of vessels. Capt. R. E. Whitehead, who had been the first to propose inland training, persuaded the navy to replace the superstructures of a pair of lake passenger steamers with flat decks. Thus, the SS *Seeandbee*, the largest passenger ship on the Great Lakes, became the USS *Wolverine*, and the SS *Badger* reemerged as the USS *Sable*. By August 1942 the first class of pilots was taking off from Glenview to perform their practice landings and takeoffs from the carriers. On clear days, Chicagoans got a perfect view of the action, including the occasional mishaps that left wrecked trainers in the lake.[31]

The three major outlying military bases were permanent and dedicated to general training, but the military also established a number of more specialized training programs that were centered nearer to downtown. Although it was already short of space, the public school system turned over facilities to the military. In June 1942 its new twenty-one-acre Chicago Vocational School became the Navy Training School for Mechanical Work, with five thousand seamen enrolled. In other parts of the city three whole school buildings were occupied by a program jointly operated with the Army Signal Corps to train radio repair personnel.[32]

University campuses, which had lost much of their male student population to the military, were easily adapted to military training at a higher level than that given general inductees.[33] ROTC units could be found on almost every campus, while programs in meteorology, navigation, code, radio, and other subjects sprouted everywhere. The University of Chicago offered one of the most intensive foreign languages programs available.[34] DePaul University virtually vacated its North Side campus to army engineering students, while rival Loyola operated the navy's V-7 programs to qualify deck officers.[35]

Northwestern University operated the largest programs, ultimately graduating forty thousand men and women from its programs. Its new Technical Institute on the Evanston campus offered preflight instruction, as well as specialized science courses. The navy took over the university's new Abbott Hall, a lakefront dormitory on the Near North Side professional schools' campus, which became the center for several nearby programs. Between September 1940 and the beginning of its last class in February 1945, Abbott Hall alone turned out sixteen thousand midshipmen. Local yacht owners volunteered their vessels for use in basic seamanship training in the adjacent lake, while the navy also took over the former Municipal Pier, where the Chicago public schools established a program to train aviation machinist mates and metalsmiths.[36]

Only a few people knew about one training program that operated in the shadow of the Water Tower in the Lewis Building at 820 North Michigan Avenue. The navy and Loyola University occupied most of the seventeen-story structure, but its top floors were occupied by the army's Counter Intelligence Corps (CIC). Every five weeks two hundred CIC agents arrived from all parts of the country to take an intensive course in detection and espionage in what was perhaps the nation's busiest spy school. Agents studied weaponry, enemy ideology, and observation techniques, as well as lock-picking.[37]

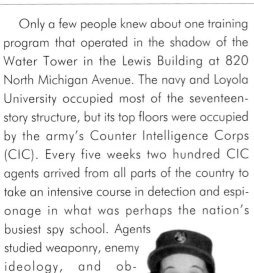

The most controversial military program involved the army's use of the three-thousand-room Stevens Hotel, the largest in the world. Built in 1927 at a cost of $26 million, it had gone bankrupt during the depression. The army saw it as a perfect place to house fifteen thousand air corps trainees. Not only did it require little remodeling, but its transportation facilities were excellent, and it was across the street from Grant Park, which could be used as a parade ground. In June 1942 the army leased the Stevens and the nearby one-thousand-room Congress Hotel for use as a radio school for its Army Air Forces Technical Training Command. In January 1943, just as the first class of radio operators graduated, the army abruptly purchased the Stevens for $6 million. But then, only three months after that, rising costs forced the army to end its nationwide program of using hotels for training purposes. Amidst fears by real estate interests that the use of the Stevens as a government office building would hurt Michigan Avenue property values, the government vacated the building August 15, 1943, and sold it a month later to a hotel corporation for $5.2 million.[38]

Downtown streets and parks, which had seen a decline in everyday traffic because of gasoline and tire rationing, seemed filled with uniformed men and women.[39] The military bureaucracy joined their civilian counterparts in the Civic Opera Building and 111 West Jackson Boulevard. The army leased the Women's Club Building, while the navy took the Woman's Athletic Club Building. The huge Hibbard, Spencer, Bartlett warehouse on North Water Street, the Carson Pirie Scott & Co. wholesale store, the Chicago Coliseum, the International Amphitheater, and some of the largest buildings in the Central Manufacturing District—all became military facilities.[40] Balaban and Katz, the movie theater chain, turned over the facilities of its new television station in the State-Lake Building to the navy for training in radar, the only such privately endowed and donated military training facility in the country.[41]

The Best Liberty Town in America

The crowds of trainees living near the Loop, along with the enormous volume of military traffic passing through the seven main downtown rail terminals, created a number of potential civil order problems. Each day, military police and shore patrol forces rode 32,022 miles on eighty-four trains in and out of the city, mostly on commuter runs serving the outlying bases. They answered questions and saw to it

Above, a soldier and his date enjoy a night on the town at one of the city's many nightclubs. Right, hostesses entertain a group of sailors at the Waukegan USO Club.

that sailors and soldiers were well-groomed, sober, and held the proper tickets.[42] The military patrols also watched for unscrupulous cab drivers and other thieves who had long preyed on unsuspecting out-of-towners by charging exorbitant fares for circuitous routes or robbing them in secluded spots.[43]

There was also a fear that prostitution and venereal disease would soar as a result of tens of thousands of military people left with nothing to do in the big city. "Prostitution is everybody's concern," noted the district supervisor of the federal Office of Social Protection in War, who advised that low wages and high rents often drove young women to the streets. Gonorrhea and syphilis rates did, in fact, increase to the point that in November 1942 the federal government opened the Chicago Venereal Disease Hospital, the nation's first specialized treatment facility.[44] Chicago remained a "wide-open town," but there was some effort to isolate the military from its seamier elements. The city health department quarantined prostitution houses, and police patrolled Grant Park, a favorite "pick-up" place for both prostitutes and young girls. Mayor Kelly reportedly hired Mrs. Loyal Davis, wife of a prominent physician, as a "liquor cop." She organized teams of underage military personnel to go into bars and ask to be served; servers who obliged ended up in court.[45]

While there were occasional problems, Chicago's preventive approach earned it the reputation as the best liberty town in America.[46] The city had begun responding to the needs of the traveling military months before Pearl Harbor. On September 5, 1941, the army established a tent camp at the corner of Foster and Kilbourn streets on the Northwest Side. Built by the Civilian Conservation Corps, the eighty-eight-tent facility was called the Chicago Recreational Area Camp and was made available for men on leave.[47] During the summer of

1941, City Hall took over a club building at 176 West Washington Steet that had been abandoned by the Elks organization and reopened it as the Chicago Service Men's Center. Volunteers outnumbered the forty-seven patrons the first night, but the idea blossomed and expanded to keep pace with the

To guard against venereal diseases, the government advised servicemen that "'No' is the best tactic . . . the next, prophylactic!"

demand, especially after the United States entered the war.[48]

As the months passed, it became clear that the volume of military personnel passing through the city exceeded all expectations, forcing an expansion of facilities. The Chicago Park District, which had made a special effort to find recreational activities for idle adults during the depression, took over operation of the Service Men's Center. In June 1942 the park district installed a summertime annex in the former Daily News Sanitarium and the small island on which it stood at the foot of Fullerton Parkway and the lakefront. In late July, the city announced that it had leased the Auditorium Building. Once Chicago's showpiece, it was bankrupt, abandoned, and derelict, but its hotel rooms and office wing were easily adapted to sleeping rooms and lounges for soldiers and sailors. Other rooms were set aside for reading, writing letters, and playing games. Some rooms featured music, which ranged from classical to popular. A row of bowling lanes was erected on the stage of its mammoth theater.[49]

There was still one remaining problem. Although black soldiers had distinguished themselves on the battlefield, they were still subjected to segregation. Even after the navy began recruiting African-Americans with some measure of equality after April 1942, black personnel lived in separate barracks and ate in separate mess halls. Things were even worse when they came to Chicago on leave or to change trains. Most Loop hotels and restaurants would not serve them. This concerned Mayor Kelly, whose efforts at integration of minorities into his political organization had made him an enormously popular figure in the so-called Black Belt. Kelly also feared conflicts that might be generated when African-Americans came into contact with southern whites. Kelly formulated a dual policy, which forbade discrimination at either of the three central centers, but also established a separate center for black soldiers on the South Side. It opened December 15, 1941, at 5111 South Calumet Avenue. Business organizations and women's clubs in the black community do-

The Lincoln Park Service Men's Center, situated at Fullerton Parkway and the lakefront, offered many activities during the summer.

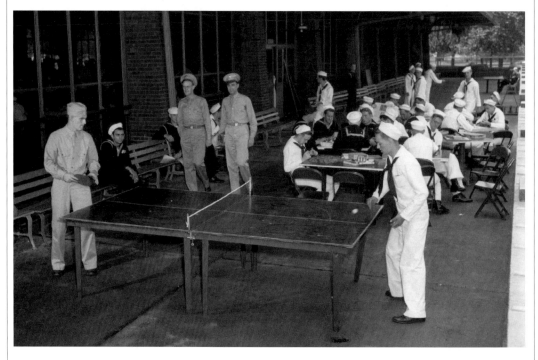

nated most of the equipment in the South Side center, which provided sleeping accommodations for fifty and a basement gym. "The Negro servicemen have always been welcome at the main Service Men's Center, 176 West Washington," commented the *Daily News*, "but although sincerely appreciative, they frankly admit they would rather be here."[50]

Chicago's Service Men's Centers were hugely successful. Attendance at the two Loop centers reached the five million mark on April 10, 1943, and thank-you letters from soldiers and sailors in foxholes and on ship bunks streamed in. One Gold Star mother from Colorado mailed in her son's last $1.60 paycheck. He had trained at the Naval Armory and had enjoyed visiting one of the centers.[51]

Although the *Civilian Defense Alert* proudly boasted that "The Service Men's Centers have coordinated and systematized entertainment for our men in uniform, replacing haphazard and sporadic individualistic efforts," they were only four of the numerous facilities available at the Chicago crossroads. The United Service

Organization (USO), established nationally in February 1941 to coordinate efforts by religious organizations, took over the task of operating the lounges and the information bureaus of the Travelers' Aid Society, one of its member organizations, at the railway stations. By January 1943, these six facilities were serving an estimated forty thousand travelers each week. Then the USO opened a twenty-thou-

Bottom, couples dance at the South Side Service Men's Center. Below, black soldiers who fought to protect democracy often faced discrimination when they returned home.

DIARY OF A RETURNING HERO

THIS SIDE FOR COLORED

"THOSE GERMAN PRISONERS WOULDN'T EAT IF I ALLOWED YOU TO SIT NEAR THEM!"

DIARY OF A RETURNING HERO

"I'D RATHER STAND-UP ALL THE WAY!"

You help someone you know... when you give to the USO

Chicagoans were reminded to support the soldiers by giving to the USO or by buying bonds.

sand-square-foot club at 131 South Wabash. It had all of the usual game equipment, plus a photographic darkroom and a tent golf driving range. In the coming months, the USO established eleven other clubs in the Chicago area, while other groups ranging from labor unions to Masonic and religious organizations joined the movement to "adopt" servicemen passing through town.[52] Approximately two thousand military women passed through Chicago each week. While not banned from the Service Men's Centers, they felt more comfortable in the Bismarck Hotel lounge created for them by the American Women's Volunteer Service.[53] No one really knows how many service personnel passed through Chicago, but when the Auditorium center closed after the war, it had served twenty-two million meals.

The Service Men's Centers, USO, and similar organizations linked the downtown crossroads and the neighborhoods. Everyone wanted to help. Volunteers sacrificed their time, money, and valuable ration coupons to produce literally hundreds of thousands of pies and cakes, as well as providing almost every other kind of food. On one Sunday alone, American Legion posts manning school cafeterias across the city cooked and served ten tons

of fried chicken. Suburban volunteers collected desserts and carried them downtown on commuter trains. Young women, all of whom had to have a letter of recommendation and a birth certificate to prove their age, poured in from the neighborhoods to sign up to serve as hostesses in one of the center's canteens. The USO's "131 Club" even issued a booklet stating the rules for hostessing.

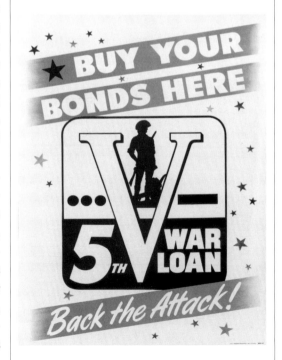

BUY YOUR BONDS HERE

5TH WAR LOAN

Back the Attack!

The function of the downtown as the central focus of homefront activities mirrored its traditional role as the center of Chicago's life during the 1940s. It was the seat of government, from which Mayor Kelly directed both city affairs and the region's civilian defense activities. From this central place of coordination, it was often difficult to differentiate between the various neighborhoods. On State Street, department stores set the styles for clothing and home furnishings. Downtown was the cultural center, as well as the entertainment district. Movies premiered in Randolph Street movie houses weeks before they were seen anywhere else. Newspapers and radio stations dispersed information and opinion from downtown. The elevated tracks and the ring of rail passenger stations, which carried both commuters and intercity travelers, defined the boundaries of the Loop.

Downtown was also the most public of the places associated with the homefront. Families nurtured the individual. Neighbors strove to get to know one another. Both had roots in similarity of class and, usually, ethnicity. But the Loop crowd was cosmopolitan and demonstrated the degree to which Chicago was an international city. Being downtown also ensured virtual anonymity that lacked any real privacy that could be invaded. Although the giant rally and the act of scraping fat into a collection container both worked for victory, they did so in different ways.

✪   ✪   ✪   ✪   ✪   ✪

Ultimately, the war in Chicago was a geographically ordered experience. Homefront activities in each part of the city grew out of the historic evolution and use of each type of area. The arena for the production war was the vast maze of industrial belts that followed along the branches of the river and the rail lines. Similarly, civilian defense activities reflected the differences between family-oriented neighborhoods, which were dominated by detached houses, and crowded apartment districts.

Inventing the Postwar World

n August 14, 1945, it was finally over. Chicagoans, who had taken to the streets to celebrate the victory over Germany on May 8, 1945, began to mark the triumph once more. Many poured into churches. Although it was midnight and raining, others hopped a streetcar or el train bound for the Loop. It was appropriate that the place where rallies that helped sustain the city's emotional unity was the place that attracted hundreds of thousands of revelers.

A blizzard of paper fell from office buildings, and conga lines danced through State Street. Surging crowds surrounded cars driven by pajama-clad revelers. Few people went home during the next day, and when word of the war's official end came at 6 P.M., the second night of celebration began. The crowd, estimated at one million by the police, filled most of State, Randolph, Washington, and Dearborn streets. Bags of water were dropped from buildings. Many firecrackers and some guns went off, but few people were hurt. Police chief Prendergast labeled it a "carnival of clean fun," in contrast with the victory celebration of 1918, which he remembered as "the rampage of a disorganized mob."[1] One naked reveler found on Michigan Avenue had only one response for the police: "Don't you know there's a war off?"[2]

Even as the celebrations began, many Chicagoans contemplated the implications of the atomic bomb that ended the war. The success of the bomb evoked boasting about Chicago's role in its creation. Some details of the Stagg Field experiment were made public,

and companies that had had the smallest part in making a tool that helped create some other tool that made a tiny part of the device claimed credit for having a major role in ending the war. At the same time, many realized the potential for world destruction that science had unleashed. In the words of one journalist, "Never in history has tea, luncheon, and dinner table conversation been so awe-inspiring, so controversial, so 'atomic.' . . . Family gatherings have become scientific discussion groups, and everyone in the family has an idea to offer."[3]

The sobering prospect of unemployment overshadowed the victory celebrations for some Chicagoans. Just as war seemed like a free-fall plunge into the unknown, peace repre-

Opposite, Chicagoans celebrate V-E and V-J days in the Loop. After the celebrations were over, soliders and civilians had to adjust to the postwar world, which included the prospect of worldwide nuclear destruction.

sented a sudden disruption of the predictable routine of war work. Optimists thought the end would not come until the official Japanese surrender, which might take weeks. Douglas Aircraft, which continued to advertise for new employees, told its workers that "the need for C-54 Skymasters is urgent," and that they would have jobs after the war. But while the crowds were still cheering downtown, Carnegie–Illinois Steel began banking three of its four large furnaces and telling workers not to show up for the next day's shift. All across the Chicago area, companies called in managers around the clock to anticipate the telegrams that would immediately cancel all war contracts.

During the next few days, the "victory lay-offs" began. On August 17, Douglas reduced its work week from forty-eight to forty hours, cut 3,348 jobs, and announced that the remaining seventeen thousand employees would be laid off when the plant closed in October. At Dodge-Chicago, half of the thirty thousand workers received immediate dismissal notices. Buick announced that it would be fully shut down by August 24. Newspapers carried cutback notices for plant after plant.[4]

Dismissed workers' responses ranged from shock to resignation. Only the naive failed to believe what they had heard all summer: the predictions of massive unemployment by Christmas. The most sanguine Chicagoans were those whose companies had already made reconversion plans. They expected only a brief layoff before returning to assembly lines to make toasters, Pullman cars, farm machinery, rail locomotives, and other consumer and producer goods. Aviation workers faced the bleakest prospects. Their plants, which were operated by out-of-town companies and often located in rented buildings, had no replacement product on the horizon. At the same time, the top wages paid aviation workers made it difficult for them to accept any of the thousands

of jobs available through the state unemployment service. Most of the latter were low-paying service-sector jobs whose original holders had fled to the defense factories.[5]

In announcing that they had a large backlog of public works projects in the wings, Mayor Kelly's public works and planning department offered a hopeful note. A new world of park buildings, expressways, housing projects, subways, and other public works would emerge from the need to create jobs to keep food on the table for thousands. City agencies had been diverting money from bond issues, motor fuel tax revenues, and city appropriations to a postwar fund that had swelled to $145 million. The only thing standing in the way of a quick start-up was the shortage of steel, lumber, and other essential materials.[6]

Many themes wound their way through the forty-four months of war. The homefront experience redefined, at least temporarily, the place of the individual in society. The war invaded the family and all of its activities with a thoroughness not seen before or since. In drawing Chicagoans to the service or the factory, it took mothers and fathers away from children. Everything the family ate or bought conformed to government rules, making technical criminals out of a huge number of Americans who found ways to cheat the system. Bond rallies and other big events, as well as the extra hours put in to help the plant win an E-Award, represented the loss of a sense of individualism.

People seemed to live an entire lifetime in less than four years. Instant marriages, the have-a-last-fling mentality, the 'round-the-clock training of workers, the speeded-up production line, the overtime hours at work—all represented a compression of time. Yet, it was also "hurry up and wait." Young couples had to postpone families, as well as housing and most consumer purchases, until after the war. The wartime emergency meant individuals' loss

The government issued this pamphlet to help veterans who planned to start their own businesses.

of power to make decisions. It is not surprising, then, that popular sociologists labeled the 1950s the decade of conformity. The marching soldier became *The Organization Man* and *The Man in the Gray Flannel Suit*. Yet the war was also a broadening experience. Workers left demoralized by the depression found high-paying jobs and learned skills that prepared them for life.

In reality, at least two homefronts existed in Chicago. During the first phase of the conflict, the level of enthusiasm and cooperation was high. Citizens seemed willing to sacrifice a measure of their freedom and convenience, perhaps in thanks for their new prosperity, but also because they genuinely believed that the city could be attacked by the enemy. Early in 1943, however, morale began to waver. Interest in scrap drives and civilian defense declined. The black market threatened the government's rationing controls. Subtle rebellions,

evident in such widely scattered areas as clothing purchases and defiant behavior among teenagers, increased. Perhaps the populace tired of the cycles of optimism and pessimism based on the defeats and triumphs on the battlefronts. American involvement in World War I lasted only about eighteen months, and many Americans expected the same duration for World War II. The change in attitude may have been rooted in the rapid growth of the military, as far more Americans were sent overseas during the last months of the war than at the beginning. Many more people were directly touched by the war in 1944 than in 1942. Mostly, however, the culprit may have been simple boredom. The fever pitch of patriotic enthusiasm for scrap drives, blackouts, and other war activities was impossible to sustain.

At the same time, the industrial world of the city changed after late 1942. Workers turned in forty-eight-hour weeks. New aircraft and elec-

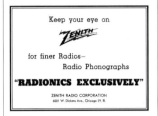
tronics plants offered employees the best pay, but since they were located on the periphery of the city, workers faced exhausting commutes. Labor recruiting brought in thousands of workers from outside the city, causing an extreme housing shortage. The growing labor deficiency also meant that virtually all of the previously unemployed, as well as large numbers of the handicapped and older workers, worked. Women and minorities accounted for the labor expansion after the end of 1942. Most African-Americans went on the job without incident, but there were cases of racial discord. And many of those who thought that women belonged in the kitchen had difficulty accepting them in the workplace. It is no coincidence that the issue of juvenile delinquency attracted its greatest wave of concern at about the same time that the major industrial recruiting drives for women began.

Besides the dramatic changes during the conflict itself, World War II planted the seeds for many changes to come. Chicago grew, and in 1950 the city's population reached 3.6 million. Most of that growth came from con-

struction of new public housing units and from new single-family housing that was built on the northwest and southwest parts of the city, which had remained undeveloped since the 1889 annexation.

Because the feared postwar depression never materialized, the construction boom benefited. In the months and years that followed, the economy suffered through strikes and inflation, as controls were lifted, but it generally rebounded to levels far beyond the most optimistic predictions. Enforced wartime saving helped fuel postwar recovery. Bond drives, paycheck deductions, bonds for infants, and savings stamps had provided an attractive alternative to spending for scarce black market goods. These funds not only served as a cushion during reconversion unemployment, but they also provided money to buy new consumer goods, visions of which had begun to appear midway through the conflict.

Unlike during the depression, no world's fairs presented a unified vision of the future. Instead, the invention of postwar America came in scattered newspaper and magazine articles that seemed to promise a technological solution to a variety of wartime social dislocations. Those who worried about the disintegration of domestic relations could take heart in the new houses that promised multipurpose living rooms more oriented to bringing the family together than to formal entertaining.[7] Kitchens would assume a new personality, and the plethora of new appliances that eased the slow job of food preparation gave their users new power. A new freezer, a kitchen with decent cabinet space, a new stove, and a washing machine and dryer promised independence in the form of greater flexibility in food purchases and convenience in doing laundry and baking in the home.[8] Meanwhile, families who were sick of slow public transit could look forward to replacing the old car with a sleek postwar model, even

War bonds helped people save for the future.

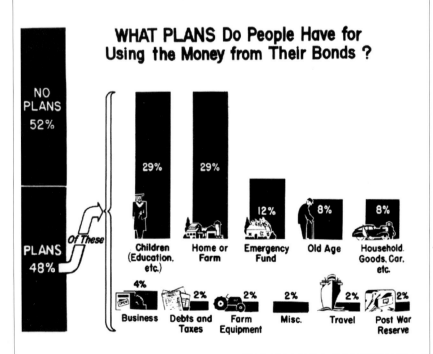

WHAT PLANS Do People Have for Using the Money from Their Bonds ?

NO PLANS 52%

PLANS 48%

Of These

29% Children (Education, etc.)

29% Home or Farm

12% Emergency Fund

8% Old Age

8% Household. Goods, Car, etc.

4% Business

2% Debts and Taxes

2% Farm Equipment

2% Misc.

2% Travel

2% Post War Reserve

though it would be 1949 before the redesigned dream cars would become reality.[9]

Ultimately, the war helped Chicago's economy gain a share in producing those consumer products. Besides the giant factories, nearly four hundred smaller plants were built because of the war, while 1,450 others expanded. But instead of a surplus of manufacturing space when the conflict ended, there was actually a shortage because of the size and speed of reconversion to consumer goods. In January 1946 Chicago-area steel plants surpassed those of Pittsburgh in production.[10] The wartime electronics industries quickly turned to the production of telephone equipment, radios, record players, and radar for civilian use. By 1950 Zenith, Admiral, Motorola, and other local producers made Chicago the nation's leading center for the production of television sets.[11] Local companies reconverted to the manufacture of everything from aluminum pressure cookers to kitchen appliances, furniture, cosmetics, and plastics.

The 1941 prediction made by some planners that war would accelerate the city's growth had come true. The sudden infusion of manufacturing capital, much of it in the form of new plants on the city's periphery, along with the fear of bombing, hastened the process of suburbanization that had already begun decades earlier. During the war, many future homeowners had also been making payments on an outlying lot instead of on one of the scarce defense houses.[12] The provisions of the 1949 Federal Housing Act accelerated the movement. Low-interest loans for veterans and others carried stipulations requiring new construction, cheap lots, and relatively low construction costs. It was financially more attractive to buy a suburban house and commute to the city job in a new postwar car than to buy the old two-flat down the street. The development of Park Forest, a planned bedroom-community thirty miles south of the Loop, gained national acclaim as a model for postwar suburban life. Expressway plans that had been drawn up as postwar relief projects would pave the way for the suburban exodus.[13]

This R. Cooper Jr. Inc. advertisement from 1945 states that "electrical equipment stands near the top in postwar wants."

A father flies a kite with his children in front of new housing in suburban Park Forest, 1951.

Postwar housing at the University of Chicago.

DO YOU WANT
YOUR WIFE
TO WORK
AFTER THE WAR
?

EM 31
G I ROUNDTABLE
★

After the war, many working women were pressured to return to their traditional roles as homemakers.

Ironically, city government helped the dispersal through the new role it envisioned for Chicago as an international aviation hub. In 1943 planners were convinced that Municipal Airport, already the nation's busiest, would soon be unable to handle both the quantity of passengers and the new types of aircraft that lay in the future. By the end of the war, magazines and newspapers overflowed with stories about the huge planes and jet-assisted takeoff, which required long runways. The newspapers and the experts examined Chicago's alternatives: an enlarged Southwest Side field, one located in the Lake Calumet wastelands, a landfill pro-

ject a few miles in the lake, and finally, the most logical alternative, the Douglas plant site, northwest of the city.[14]

Local officials joined several airlines in lobbying for Chicago to become an international terminus.[15] That dream was realized on November 14, 1945, when Mayor Kelly climbed aboard the first overseas flight to take off from the city. His destination was London, where he made a plea for the United Nations to locate its new world headquarters on the lakefront site of the A Century of Progress Exposition.[16] That mission failed, but a new lakefront airport named after Merrill Meigs, Chicago's first aviation commissioner, rose on the spot. It handled smaller planes, while the city's eventual replacement for Municipal Airport took another seven years to complete. On September 18, 1949, it was named O'Hare International Airport in honor of Edward H. "Butch" O'Hare, a St. Louis-born air hero whom Chicago adopted as its own.[17]

Months before the conflict ended, many working women were pressured to leave their jobs when peace came. Some women happily relinquished them to returning veterans, preferring instead to raise the long-deferred family in the long-awaited house. Other women resisted the idea of giving up the skills they had studied and trained so hard to obtain, let alone the extra income that could buy the postwar goods.[18]

The experience was even more frustrating for African-Americans. They realized that the old "last hired, first fired" adage applied most to their community, which had faced discrimination even during the most extreme labor shortages. Stories about impending layoffs warranted more space in the *Defender* than did news of victory celebrations. Yet the war was a turning point for black Chicagoans. Despite the difficulties that African-Americans encountered in getting war jobs, the city became a beacon of prosperity to black southerners.

The size of the city's black community grew from 277,731 in 1940 to 492,265 a decade later. Returning black vets not only provided the new business leadership for their community, but the war experience both in the service and at home fueled a new demand for equality that grew into the civil rights movement of the 1950s and 1960s. Politically, the black community demanded and received a larger share of city jobs and influence, while memories of wartime prosperity helped drive the growing demand for equality that quickly surfaced.[19] In September 1945 charges of racial discrimination against the Central YMCA College led to a walkout of faculty and students that resulted in the formation of Roosevelt College, which took over the Auditorium Building. Ironically, many of the veterans who had once stopped there when it was a servicemen's center returned as students in the new university.[20]

The spirit that created Roosevelt College was typical of both the vigor and the quest for education and training that vets brought back with them when they returned to Chicago. Dozens of new businesses bore the names "Victory" or "Veteran's." Many veterans took advantage of the GI Bill to attend college. The two-year campus of the University of Illinois, which occupied a portion of Navy Pier, was familiar territory for many former sailors. Meanwhile, the huge new Vaughn Hospital at Hines, near Maywood, was rushed to completion in anticipation of growing need to treat wounded veterans.[21]

Half a century has now passed since the news of Pearl Harbor crackled over the living room radio, but the war is still with us. It is here in the form of places and buildings. Walk half a block west from "Victory Plaza," the west face of City Hall, and you will find 176 West Washington Street looking almost exactly as it did when it was Service Men's Center #1. Center #2, the Auditorium Building, is now home of Roosevelt University. Only the main waiting room of Union Station survives to remind us of when that place was Chicago's rail hub. Municipal Airport lives on as Midway Airport, renamed in 1949 to commemorate the Battle of Midway. Abbott Hall of Northwestern University and what is left of Navy Pier still face each other across Lake Shore Drive, up the road a few miles from Soldier Field. Out at the University of Chicago, the west stands of Stagg Field are gone. A symbolic statue by Henry Moore occupies the site. At the Illinois Institute of Technology, Armour Hall remains as a symbol of that institution's contributions to the war effort.

Many of the industrial plants erected during the war are still busy, though the biggest are either gone or have some new use. The Douglas plant, which stood on what is now the military side of O'Hare, is gone, but the Studebaker building is a warehouse, while Amertorp and Dodge-Chicago went through several uses before being recycled into Forest Park Mall and Ford City Shopping Center, respectively. Some of the memorial plaques still look down on intersections, while special monuments dot cemeteries and parks in memory of the seventeen thousand Illinois residents who died in the war.

Most important of all, the war is still with us in our human links with the era, although each passing decade has changed our perspective by removing the oldest surviving groups. Most of those who were approaching middle or old age are gone, many of them parents who died with the painful memory of the dreaded telegram informing them of the loss of a son or daughter. The military sacrifices of wartime Chicagoans, their superhuman effort in the defense plant, their patriotic willingness to do without, and their realization that fairness and unity were needed—all of these cannot help but evoke a sense of awe from the generations of Chicagoans that have followed.

Notes

Abbreviations

Airview News	Douglas–Chicago Airview News
CDA	Civilian Defense Alert
CHS	Chicago Historical Society
Daily News	Chicago Daily News
Defender	Chicago Defender
Herald-American	Chicago Herald-American
OWI	Office of War Information
OCD	Office of Civilian Defense
Sun	Chicago Sun
Times	Chicago Times
Tribune	Chicago Tribune

Introduction

1. Perry R. Duis and Glen E. Holt, "FDR and the Outer Drive Bridge," *Chicago* 31 (January 1982):104–107.
2. Mary Watters, *Illinois in the Second World War* (Springfield, Ill.: Illinois State Historical Library, 1952), II:15–21.
3. This greatly simplifies the complex story told in an excellent volume, James C. Schneider, *Should America Go to War? The Debate Over Foreign Policy in Chicago, 1939–41* (Chapel Hill: University of North Carolina Press, 1989).
4. John Tebbel, *The Marshall Fields: A Study in Wealth* (New York: E. P. Dutton & Co., 1947) 224–60.

The Household War

1. Lloyd Wendt, "What Experts Say About War Marriages," *Chicago Tribune Magazine*, Feb. 1, 1942; *Chicago Tribune Magazine*, June 4, 1942; *Daily News*, Dec. 20, 1941, Oct. 2, 1943.
2. A shortage of new products prompted many Americans to give antiques as wedding gifts. *Daily News*, March 27, 1943, June 6, 1944.
3. *Daily News*, Jan. 19, 1943.
4. *Daily News*, Oct. 11, 1943.
5. *Daily News*, Jan. 31, 1944; *Tribune*, March 12, 1945.
6. *Tribune*, June 12, 1944.
7. *Daily News*, Dec. 19, 1941; *Tribune*, Jan. 12, Feb. 12, 18, March 18, 21, May 10, 1942, June 5, 12, 1944.
8. Where 150,000 conventional letters weighed 2,575 pounds and required thirty-seven mailbags, the same correspondence on V-mail weighed only forty-five pounds and required one bag. Judy Barrett Litoff and David C. Smith, "'Will He Get My Letter?' Popular Portrayals of Mail and Morale During World War II," *Journal of Popular Culture* 23 (Spring 1990):21–45; *Daily News*, June 19, 1942, May 27, 1943, *Tribune*, Dec. 10, 1944.
9. *Tribune*, July 2, Dec. 31, 1944.
10. *CDA* 2 (Jan. 20, 1943):3.
11. Wendt, "What Experts Say About War Marriages."
12. See the series in *Daily News*, June 3–5, 1943; see also, *Daily News*, June 24, Sept. 8, Oct. 21, Nov. 16, 1943; *Tribune*, June 30, Nov. 10, Dec. 23, 1944, Jan. 26, 1945.
13. *Tribune*, Jan. 14, Feb. 6, 1942.
14. *Economist* 107 (April 18, 1942):6; *Economist* 107 (April 18, 1942):1.
15. Johnson & Johnson, which already had a 98 percent female work force, erected a circus tent on the front lawn of its factory at 4951 West Sixty-eighth Street. Employees demonstrated the products and discussed the merits of working there. *Daily News*, May 19, June 2, 4, July 2, Sept. 22, Oct. 15, 1943.
16. *Daily News*, Feb. 3, 16, 24, 1944; *Tribune*, June 9, 22, 25, 1944.
17. Another 40 percent of all live births were to first-time mothers between the ages of twenty and twenty-nine. Most of the rest were women having a second or third child because their families could now afford it. A small percentage were teenagers having their first child. *Tribune*, Sept. 5, 1944.
18. Peggy Tagliere, interview with CHS staff, April 9, 1991. Mrs. Tagliere participated in a focus group that discussed the experience of children during World War II.
19. *Tribune*, Feb. 1, 1942.
20. *Daily News*, Dec. 16, 20, 1941, Nov. 19, 1943.

21. *Daily News,* April 22, 1943.

22. *Daily News,* July 1, 1942, March 17, 1943.

23. *Daily News,* April 27, 1943.

24. *Tribune,* July 2, 1944.

25. *Daily News,* March 18, 1943; *Airview News* 1 (Oct. 12, 1943):n.p.; "Report of the Activities of the Women's Division," Jan. 1945, minutes files, Illinois War Council Papers, Illinois State Archives, Springfield, Illinois.

26. Watters, I:350–54; *Daily News,* Feb. 20, May 6, July 6, 26, 28, Dec. 9, 1943, Feb. 3, 18, 19, 1944; *Sun,* Nov. 28, 1943; *Tribune,* Dec. 10, 1944, Jan. 28, Feb. 4, 1945; *CDA* 2 (March 10, 1943):7.

27. *Daily News,* March 18, 1943; *Tribune,* June 26, July 2, 1944, Feb. 19, March 27, 28, 1945.

28. *Daily News,* May 22, June 5, Aug. 10, Oct. 15, Nov. 12, 1943, Jan. 8, Aug. 27, 1944.

29. *Daily News,* Jan. 11, 14, 1943.

30. *Daily News,* Nov. 9, 1943.

31. *Daily News,* Nov. 17, 1943.

32. *Daily News,* Feb. 25, 1943.

33. *Daily News,* Feb. 25, Sept. 23, 1943.

34. *Daily News,* Nov. 17, 1943.

35. *Daily News,* Jan. 14, Feb. 25, 1943.

36. *Daily News,* Nov. 5, 1943, Jan. 11, 19, 1944; *Tribune,* Dec. 18, 1944, Jan. 11, Feb. 28, 1945.

37. *Economist* 108 (Oct. 10, 1942):6.

38. *Economist* 108 (July 11, 1942):3; Calvin Alexander, "Savings and Loan Business Now 'Big Leaguer'" *Commerce* 39 (March 1942):25.

39. *Commerce* 39 (March 1942):32–34; *Daily News,* June 12, 1942.

40. For example, many consumers rushed out to buy stoves. The sleek new steel models were sold out by mid-1942 and were not available again until mid-1944, when the federal government began to ease restrictions. *Economist* 107 (May 16, 1942):15; *Economist* 108 (Sept. 26, 1943):28; *Daily News,* Jan. 12, 1944; *Tribune,* Aug. 12, 16, Sept. 19, 1944.

41. *Tribune,* Feb. 7, 11, March 8, 1942.

42. *Daily News,* March 27, 1942, Feb. 1, 1943, May 29, 1944; Minutes, June 16, 1943, Illinois War Council Papers, 3.

43. *Tribune,* March 19, 20, May 2, June 5, 1942, May 25, 1943; *Business Week,* April 18, 1942, 33; *Daily News,* July 17, 1943.

44. *Tribune,* Feb. 22, March 4, 28, 1942; *Daily News,* Feb. 8, May 17, 1943.

45. *Tribune,* Jan. 3, 1942; *Business Week,* April 18, 1942, 30, May 16, 1942, 50; *Daily News,* July 6, 1942, Jan. 2, April 1, Sept. 16, 1943.

46. *Business Week,* Aug. 1, 1942, 50, 53; *Business Week,* Jan. 30, 1943, 51–52; *Business Week,* July 17, 1943, 85–86; *Daily News,* July 1, 1943.

47. Watters, I:330, 339, 341; *Daily News,* May 24, 26, 1943; *Tribune,* Nov. 2, 1944.

48. Watters, II:57–58; *Daily News,* Aug. 6, 1943; *CDA* 1 (June 9, 1942):5; "Digest of Meeting Held at Council Chambers," Nov. 13, 1941, miscellaneous meetings folder, Illinois War Council Papers.

49. *Daily News,* Dec. 11, 1944.

50. *Tribune,* March 27, 1942.

51. *Tribune,* Feb. 24, March 4, 22, 27, May 1–8, 1942.

52. *Economist* 107 (Jan. 24, 1942):20; see also Coca-Cola ad, *Tribune,* Feb. 9, 1942.

53. *Tribune,* March 25, 1942.

54. *Tribune,* Feb. 27, 1942.

55. *Tribune,* March 20, 1942, *Daily News,* Feb. 2, 28, March 1, 1943.

56. *CDA* 1 (Oct. 28, 1942):1; *CDA* 1 (Nov. 25, 1942):1, 2; *CDA* 2 (Dec. 9, 1942):7.

57. *Daily News,* March 24, 26, 27, 28, 30, 1943.

58. Watters, I:338–39; *Tribune,* May 1, 1942; *Daily News,* March 4, June 12, 1943.

59. *Daily News,* April 19, 1943; *Business Week,* May 22, 1943, 14; *Business Week,* April 10, 1943, 57.

60. Some familiar packaging disappeared. *Tribune* columnist India Moffett reminded readers that, "there will be no more butter in crocks, Madam, and no more crackers in tin cans, the creamery man and the grocer say." *Tribune,* Jan. 21, 1942.

61. *Tribune,* May 1, June 7, 1942, March 28, 1945; *Daily News,* Feb. 2, 4, March 16, July 17, 1943.

62. *Daily News,* Dec. 18, 1943. The Chicago Nutrition Committee changed its name to the Chicago Nutrition Association in 1946. Chicago Nutrition Committee, Annual Report, May 1, 1943 to July 1, 1945, in Chicago Nutrition Association Papers, University of Illinois at Chicago. Douglas Bukowski, "Praise the War Food Administration and Pass the Spongette: Wartime Nutrition, 1942–1945," unpublished paper, 1978.

63. *Tribune,* Jan. 22, 26, 29, 1942; *Herald-American,* Oct. 8, 1942.

64. *Daily News,* Dec. 27, 1941, Feb. 22, 23, March 1, April 10, 14, May 6, 20, Nov. 17, 1943.

65. *CDA* 1 (March 18, 1942):3; *Commerce* 39 (Feb. 1942):7; *Tribune,* Jan.

10, 16, Feb. 22, 24, 1942; *Daily News,* Feb. 20, 22, 26, 1943.

66. Watters, I:324–26, 329, 335, 341; *Daily News,* March 19, May 10, July 16, Sept. 7, Oct. 26, 1943.

67. *Daily News,* Jan. 13, 15, Feb. 18, 19, 22, 26, April 5, 6, 27, 1943; *Tribune,* June 3, July 2, Oct. 26, Nov. 3, 1944, Feb. 16, March 21, 1945; *Business Week,* June 19, 1943.

68. *Tribune,* July 16, Dec. 24, 1944, Jan. 17, March 9, 10, 11, 12, 13, 17, 28, 1945.

69. Minutes, Jan. 22, 1945, Illinois War Council Papers, 3–4.

70. *Daily News,* Jan. 23, March 8, 1943, May 22, 1944.

71. *Daily News,* Jan. 4, Feb. 23, May 12, Aug. 3, 1943; *Tribune,* Feb. 27, May 1, 1942, July 18, 28, 1944; Watters, II:60.

72. *Daily News,* Dec. 1, 1941.

73. Richard R. Lingeman, *Don't You Know There's A War On?* (New York: G. P. Putnam, 1970), 67–68, 128; *Tribune,* Jan. 2, 3, Feb. 1, March 1, 14, 15, 1942.

74. *Daily News,* Dec. 20, 23, 27, 30, 1941; *Tribune,* Jan. 1, 2, 3, 4, 5, 6, 7, 17, 1942.

75. *Tribune,* Jan. 3, 4, 5, 6, 1942.

76. *Daily News,* Dec. 30, 1941; *Tribune,* March 1, 1942; Richard Polenberg, *War and Society: The United States, 1941–1945* (Philadelphia: J. B. Lippincott, 1972), 16–17.

77. *Daily News,* June 6, 1942; *Tribune,* Feb. 1, 1942.

78. *Daily News,* Dec. 27, 1941, May 10, June 6, 1942, Jan. 21, 1943.

79. *Daily News,* April 9, 12, July 2, 16, 1943, May 3, 1944; *Tribune,* Feb. 15, March 12, 24, 28, 1942.

80. *Business Week,* Nov. 21, 1942; *Daily News,* March 25, 1943.

81. *Tribune* Jan. 12, 1942; *Economist* 108 (Dec. 5, 1942):13.

82. Chicago Plan Commission, *Chicago Land Use Survey: General Residential Data by Quarter Square Mile.* (Chicago: Chicago Plan Commission, 1941).

83. *Tribune,* May 1, 10; *Economist* 107 (June 27, 1942):1; *Economist* 108 (Aug. 8, 1942):13; *Economist* 108 (Aug. 15, 1942):1, 5; *Economist* 108 (Aug. 22, 1942):1; *Economist* 108 (Sept. 19, 1942):1.

84. *Economist* 108 (Oct. 17, 1942):9; *Economist* 109 (Jan. 2, 1943):1; *Economist* 109 (Jan. 9, 1943):1; *Daily News,* Jan. 9, June 5, 1943.

85. *Tribune,* May 24, June 14, 1942; *Daily News,* May 8, June 19, 1943. The weekly building permits column in the *Economist* list hundreds of these conversions.

86. *Daily News,* Sept. 4, Dec. 18, 1943; *Tribune,* Aug. 6, 1944.

87. The best source for the history of the CHA is Devereux Bowly, *The Poorhouse: Subsidized Housing in Chicago, 1895–1976* (Carbondale: Southern Illinois University Press, 1978).

88. *Economist* 107 (Feb. 21, 1942):9; *Economist* 107 (May 23, 1942):28; *Economist* 108 (Aug. 29, 1942):28; *Economist* 109 (Jan. 16, 1943):6; *Economist* 110 (Oct. 2, 1943):14; *Economist* 110 (Oct. 30, 1943):20; *Economist* 110 (Dec. 18, 1943):6; see also, CHA Cabrini Homes application and handbill with letter from Harry A. White, CHA, to William H. Spence, regional director, War Manpower Commission, Feb. 5, 1943, War Man-power Commission files, Record Group 211, Box 2519, Folder 533.14, Federal Records Center, Chicago.

89. *Daily News,* June 22, 24, 1942, March 20, 1943.

90. Watters, II:304; *Daily News,* June 24, 1942, Sept. 22, 1943, May 5, 23, 1944; *Tribune,* June 25, Aug. 6, 1944.

91. *Tribune,* March 25, 26, 1942; *Daily News,* June 13, 17, 1942; *Economist* 107 (March 28, 1942):1; *Economist* 108 (July 25, 1942):10; *Economist* 108 (Aug. 8, 1942):5; *Economist* 108 (Sept. 26, 1942):6.

92. Watters, II:304; see building permit lists in *Economist;* on Oriole Park Village, see "Unified Neighborhood Development Success," *American City* 60 (Nov. 1945):110, and *Airview News* 1 (June 29, 1943):10.

93. On Douglas housing other than Oriole Park Village, see *Daily News,* March 11, Aug. 7, Sept. 25, 30, 1943; *Economist* 108 (Aug. 8, 1942):1; *Economist* 110 (Aug. 21, 1943):9; *Economist* 110 (Aug. 28, 1943):7. There are also many stories in the *Airview News,* but see especially 1 (June 15, 1943):2 and 1 (Oct. 26, 1943):1. On Dodge–Chicago, see *Tribune,* July 30, 1944, *Daily News,* April 24, May 1, 1943; *Economist* 108 (Oct. 31, 1943):1; *Economist* 108 (Dec. 5, 1943):6; *Economist* 109 (May 15, 1943):13. On J. E. Merrion and Merrionette Park, see *Daily News,* March 26, 1943, and *Economist* 106 (Oct. 18, 1941):25. On Buick, see *Tribune,* May 17, 1942, Sept. 10, 1944; *Daily News,* June 12, 1943; *Economist* 108 (July 11, 1942):15.

There are hundreds of newspaper articles and building permit listings, too numerous to mention, on suburban defense housing in Cicero, Elmhurst, Ivanhoe, Palos Heights, Lyons, River Forest, Lincolnwood, Elmhurst, Prospect Heights, Brookfield, Skokie, Bellwood, and Evanston.

94. *CDA* 1 (Sept. 29, 1942):1, 3; *CDA* 2 (Feb. 24, 1943):1; *CDA* 2 (March 17, 1943):1

95. *CDA* 1 (Oct. 7, 1942):1.

96. *Daily News,* Feb. 3, 1943.

The Neighborhood War

1. According to 1940 census figures for the 4,569,643 people in the Chicago metropolitan area, excluding Indiana, a total of 672,705 (19.8 percent) of Chicago's 3,396,808 people were foreign-born, as were 152,489 (15.3 percent) of the 995,069 people in the suburban areas within the state of Illinois. There were 277,731 (8.2 percent) African-Americans within the city and another 24,788 (2.5 percent) in the suburbs. The 4,413 (0.1 percent) city dwellers and 489 (0.05 percent) suburbanites who were classified by the census as "other than white or Negro" were primarily Asian-Americans.

2. Lingeman, *Don't You Know There's a War On?*, 34–36; Philip Funigiello, *The Challenge to Urban Liberalism: Federal-City Relations During World War II* (Knoxville: University of Tennessee Press, 1978), 48–52.

3. Watters, I:36–41.

4. Watters, I:10, 35, 40, 47.

5. Watters, I:73–74; *Tribune,* Jan. 7, 1942; see organizational charts, miscellaneous collection, OCD Papers, CHS Library.

6. Office of War Information, Bureau of Intelligence, "Chicago: Notes on Community Structure," Dec. 1942, typescript, record group 44, box 1839, OWI files, National Archives, Washington, D.C., 2–4. The author is indebted to D'Ann Campbell and Richard Jensen for calling attention to these sources.

7. *Daily News,* Dec. 19, 1942.

8. *Daily News,* Dec. 20, 1942.

9. *CDA* 2 (Jan. 13, 1943):7.

10. *Tribune,* Oct. 6, 1944.

11. *CDA* 1 (March 11, 1942):3; *CDA* 1 (April 21, 1942):1; *CDA* 1 (Sept. 29, 1942):3; *CDA* 1 (Oct. 28, 1942):1; *CDA* (Nov. 18, 1942):2.

12. *Daily News,* Dec. 31, 1941.

13. *CDA* 1 (March 18, 1942):1, 2; *CDA* 1 (March 24, 1942):1; *CDA* 1 (March 31, 1942):1, 2; *CDA* 1 (April 14, 1942):1; Watters, I:78.

14. *CDA* 2 (Dec. 30, 1942):1.

15. *CDA* 1 (March 11, 1942):2.

16. Illustrated in *Daily News,* Dec. 9, 1943, and *Business Week,* Aug. 15, 1942, 18.

17. *CDA* 2 (March 17, 1943):2; *CDA* 2 (Dec. 16, 1942):1; "Films Available for Booking Through Division Chiefs and Community Commanders" miscellaneous box 1, OCD Papers.

18. *CDA* 1 (March 24, 1942):2.

19. *CDA* 1 (March 11, 1942):1; *CDA* 1 (May 9, 1942):4. Various neighborhood publications included *The Block Club News* (Beverly), *Communique* (Jackson Park), *Block 8 News* (1800 block of Humboldt Boulevard), *Our Block Bulletin* (500 block of South Kedvale), *The News Weekly* (Hegewisch), and *War Effort Bulletin* (Indian Boundary). Listings are from

various issues of *CDA* from the summer of 1942.

20. Watters, I:75–76; *CDA* 1 (March 11, 1942):1.

21. *Tribune,* Feb. 5, 1942. Mrs. Johnson's claim that she was the first female block captain was challenged by several others. *Tribune,* Feb. 6, 1942.

22. *CDA* 1 (March 31, 1942):2.

23. In another black neighborhood, captain Joree Marshall's block pledged four thousand dollars in war bonds, contributed eight thousand pounds of salvage, collected eight hundred books for distribution to servicemen, and turned in an average of seventy-five pounds of fat and drippings to local butchers. *CDA* 1 (April 28, 1942):2; *CDA* 1 (June 16, 1942):2; *CDA* 1 (Oct. 21, 1942):3.

24. *Daily News,* June 15, 1942.

25. *Tribune,* May 2, 1942; *Economist* 107 (Jan. 10, 1942):7; on Western Electric, see *Microphone* 17 (March 1942):2; see also, *Blackout . . . Control Commercial Lighting* (Chicago: Office of Civilian Defense, Chicago Metropolitan Area, 1942) and "Inventory of Illuminated Signs and Decorative Lighting," both in miscellaneous collection, OCD Papers.

26. *Tribune,* March 19, 1942.

27. *Tribune,* March 19, 1942.

28. Not to be confused with *Civilian Defense Alert,* the city journal. See *Civilian Defense,* 1 (May 1942). Light tests are described in *Commerce* 39 (April 1942):8.

29. *Daily News,* Dec. 20, 1941, June 10, 16, Oct. 8, 9, 1942; *Tribune,* Feb. 25, 1942; *CDA* 1 (March 11, 1942):1; *CDA* 1 (April 7, 1942):1; *CDA* 1 (April 21, 1942):1; *CDA* (May 19, 1942):2;

CDA 1 (June 23, 1942):4; CDA 1 (Sept. 1, 1942):4; CDA 1 (Oct. 7, 1942):1; CDA 1 (Oct. 21, 1942):1

30. *Sun,* Aug. 13, 1942.

31. *Blackout Ordinance and Proclamation* (Chicago: Office of Civilian Defense, Chicago Metropolitan Area, 1942); "Manual for Practice Blackout, Aug. 12, 1942," miscellaneous collection, OCD Papers; CDA 1 (Aug. 18, 1942):1, 6; CDA 1 (Sept. 8, 1942):4–5, 7; *Tribune,* Aug. 11–13, 1942; *Daily News,* Aug. 10–13; *Sun,* Aug. 13, 1942.

32. *Instructions to Block Captains,* miscellaneous collection, OCD Papers; CDA 1 (Sept. 29, 1942):1; *Daily News,* Oct. 7, 8, 1942.

33. *Sun,* May 24, 1943; see also, *Tribune, Daily News, Times,* and *Herald-American* of that date; on preparations, see CDA 2 (May 5, 1943):1; CDA 2 (May 12, 1943):4–5; see also correspondence and the detailed "General Report of the Mock-Air-Raid Incident Drill of Sunday," May 23, 1943, in the miscellaneous collection, OCD Papers.

34. *Tribune,* May 16, 18, June 11, 1942; *Daily News,* June 23, 29, 30, July 1, 1942, Feb. 22, March 15, May 10, 14, 17, July 3, Oct. 21, 1943, May 23, 1944.

35. The most convenient summary of the case is Francis X. Busch, *They Escaped the Hangman* (Indianapolis: Bobbs-Merrill, 1953).

36. *Tribune,* June 1, 1942; CDA 1 (July 21, 1942):2.

37. *Tribune,* Dec. 31, 1943.

38. CDA 1 (May 26, 1942):1.

39. *Daily News,* June 3, 12, 17, 1942.

40. The draft, consumers, CDA 1 (March 24, 1942):2; sand, CDA 1 (April 28, 1942):4; binoculars, CDA 1 (Aug. 4, 1942):6; consumers, CDA 1 (Aug. 25, 1942):1; old radios, CDA 1 (Sept. 9, 1942):4; and CDA 1 (Oct. 28, 1942):4.

41. CDA 1 (April 14, 1942):2.

42. Despite an increase in manufacturing, each month of 1942 saw a decrease in the number of fires from the 1941 figures, in large part because OCD watch programs made Chicago, in the words of the *CDA,* "a safer place to live." Quote from CDA 1 (Aug. 25, 1942):2; see also, CDA 1 (March 11, 1942):1; CDA 1 (July 21, 1942):2; CDA 1 (July 28, 1942):2; CDA 1 (Aug. 11, 1942):2; CDA 2 (May 12, 1943):2; CDA 2 (Aug. 13, 1943):2.

43. Watters, I:98; Victor Kleber, *Selective Service in Illinois, 1940–1947* (Springfield: State of Illinois, 1948) 331–407, 411–12, 433–34.

44. *Daily News,* July 16, 1943; CDA 2 (Feb. 24, 1943):4.

45. CDA 1 (Nov. 18, 1942):2.

46. Watters, I:312; CDA 1 (Nov. 18, 1942):2.

47. On Boy Scouts, see *Tribune,* March 3, 8, 19, 1942; *Daily News,* Jan. 26, 1944, and especially the column, "Helping Boy Scouts Not Compulsory," in *Daily News,* Feb. 12, 1944; on Girl Scouts, see *Tribune,* Jan. 17, 26, Feb. 17, 20, 21, March 1, 26, 27, 1942, and especially, "Girl Scouts Seek Wider Usefulness," *Daily News,* June 3, 1944; On Camp Fire Girls, see *Tribune,* March 26, 1942.

48. *How to Serve Your Community, American Youth Reserves,* pamphlet in miscellaneous collection, OCD

Papers; CDA 1 (June 9, 1942):13; CDA 2 (Dec. 9, 1942):2; CDA 2 (May 5, 1943):3; CDA 2 (Oct. 22, 1943):1; *Daily News,* Feb. 25, 1943.

49. CDA 2 (June 2, 1943):4; CDA 2 (July 9, 1943):2.

50. CDA 2 (July 1943):8; CDA 2 (Sept. 1943):3.

51. Quoted in CDA 1 (April 14, 1942):2; Watters, I:280–91; see also small collection in OCD Papers.

52. Duis and Holt, "FDR and the Outer Drive Bridge."

53. Despite the late start, 12,601 registered gardeners cultivated 508 public plots totaling about 290 acres within the city limits during the 1942 season. The OCD estimated that this amounted to less than one third of the total within the city. The following year the number gardens reached 145,000; 59,247 of these were officially registered. In the latter year nineteen hundred cultivated acres produced more than fifty thousand tons of food. "Report of the Victory Garden Department, Office of Civilian Defense, Chicago Metropolitan Area, for the period from its inception in 1941 to December 31, 1943," mimeo, OCD Papers; *How to Grow a Victory Garden in the Chicago Metropolitan Area* (Chicago: Office of Civilian Defense, 1943); Watters, I:283; CDA 2 (Oct. 1943):3.

54. On Feb. 22, 1942, the *Tribune* first published a map that showed growing districts based on smoke; *How to Grow a Victory Garden,* 8–9.

55. *Tribune,* March 8, 1942; *Airview News,* 1 (Aug. 17, 1943):4.

56. The "How to Make a Victory Garden" column first appeared in the *Tribune* on Jan. 19, 1942. See also the Fair ad on

back cover of the 1943 edition of *How to Grow a Victory Garden*.

57. Watters, I:291; *Daily News*, March 1, 1943; *Tribune*, March 9, 1945.

58. Watters, I:289; *Economist* 110 (Aug. 28, 1943):28; *Daily News*, July 10, 1943.

59. The newspapers frequently told stories of cooperation. See *Tribune*, May 3, 1942, June 4, 1942; *CDA* 1 (July 14, 1942):2

60. *CDA* 2 (Oct. 14, 1942):2.

61. *CDA* 1 (Aug. 25, 1942):3; *CDA* 1 (Oct. 14, 1942):2; *Economist* 108 (July 11, 1942):31.

62. *Economist* 110 (Aug. 28, 1943):28; *CDA* 2 (May 12, 1943):2.

63. Illinois War Council Conservation Committee Minutes, May 8, 1944, and July 10, 1944, Illinois War Council Papers, n.p.; *Daily News*, March 30, 1944; *Tribune*, Feb. 18, 1945.

64. *Daily News*, Dec. 18, 1941.

65. The Chicago and North Western responded to a letter from the editor, *Tribune*, Jan. 12, 1942; see also, *Tribune*, Feb. 20, 1942.

66. Trade associations also cooperated. The Cleaners and Dyers of Chicago established uniform policies that required customers to return hangers with incoming orders, eliminated paper bags, and reduced delivery schedules. The Chicago Motor Club sent 10,775 individual pledge cards to members, asking them to search their garages for useful salvage. *Tribune*, March 8, 14, 1942; "Renew Golf Balls," *Business Week*, April 11, 1947, 54, 57; *CDA* 1 (July 7, 1942):3.

67. "Co-operation of Chainstores in Scrap Drive," March, 1942, file, Illinois War Council Papers.

68. *Tribune*, Feb. 12, 1942.

69. *CDA* 1 (March 31, 1942):1; *CDA* 1 (July 7, 1942):3; *Tribune*, Feb. 27, March 2, 1942.

70. *CDA* 1 (Nov. 18, 1942):2.

71. *Tribune*, Feb. 12, 25, 1942.

72. *Tribune*, Jan. 6, 1942.

73. *CDA* 1 (April 28, 1942):1; *CDA* 1 (June 9, 1942):5; *Daily News*, June 23, 1942.

74. "A Quiz on Vital Home Defense Need of Saving Home Kitchen Greases," mimeo, OCD Papers; *Daily News*, June 24, 1942.

75. *Tribune*, June 14, 1942.

76. *Daily News*, June 12, 18, July 1, 1942; *Tribune*, Dec. 12, 1942.

77. *CDA* 1 (March 11, 1942):3; *CDA* 1 (July 14, 1942):7; *CDA* 1 (Dec. 9, 1942):2; *Daily News*, June 3, 1942; *Tribune*, June 10, 1942.

78. *CDA* 1 (July 14, 1942):5.

79. *CDA* 1 (Sept. 29, 1942):2; *CDA* 1 (Nov. 4, 1942):1; *Economist* 108 (Oct. 17, 1942):28.

80. *CDA* 2 (Dec. 9, 1942):3.

81. *CDA* 2 (Feb. 10, 1943):7; *Daily News*, Feb. 12, 1943.

82. *Daily News*, April 8, Oct. 23, Dec. 13, 1943; Illinois War Council Minutes, March 6, 1944, Illinois War Council Papers, 5.

83. *Tribune*, July 4, Aug. 3, Nov. 13, 1944.

84. *Daily News*, Dec. 31, 1943, Jan. 3, 6 (cartoon), 12, 15, 18, June 5, 1944; *Tribune*, Jan. 16, 1944; *Sun*, Jan. 15, 21, 1944; see also, collection of postcards, programs, forms, and notices in CHS Library.

85. *Daily News*, June 5, 1944; *Tribune*, June 19, 21, 23, Aug. 8, 13, 1944; Watters, I:267.

86. The region is mapped in *CDA* 1 (March 18, 1942):2.

87. *CDA* 1 (June 16, 1942):5; *CDA* 1 (May 1942):8–10.

88. *Tribune*, March 8, 1942.

89. *Daily News*, July 10, 1943.

90. *CDA* 1 (March 18, 1942):3; *CDA* 1 (March 24, 1942):3.

91. *Tribune*, March 8, 1942.

92. Annette Bender, "Civilian Defense Block Organization in Hyde Park" (Master's thesis, University of Chicago, 1943)

93. *CDA* 1 (Aug. 11, 1942):8; *Daily News*, Oct. 29, Nov. 22, 1943; June 23, 1945.

94. *Tribune*, Dec. 9, 1944.

95. *Daily News*, Jan. 4, 1944; *Tribune*, July 6, 1944.

96. OWI, Bureau of Intelligence, "Tensions in the Chicago Area, Week of January 18–23, [1943]," record group 44, box 1839, OWI files.

97. *Tribune*, April 27, May 11, 18, 25, June 1, 15, 1942; *Daily News*, Aug. 12, 30, 1943.

98. *Tribune*, April 27, May 4, 11, 25, June 1, 15, 1942.

99. *Tribune*, Oct. 1, 1941, May 25, June 14, 1942.

100. *Daily News*, Jan. 12, 1944.

101. Pittsburgh *Courier*, Jan. 11, 1940.

102. *Defender*, July 3, 1943; *Daily News*, April 29, 1943.

103. *Daily News*, Dec. 20, 1941.

104. The classic study of black Chicago during this period is St. Clair Drake and Horace Cayton, *Black Metropolis: A Study of Negro Life in a Northern City* (New York: Harcourt, Brace, 1945).

105. *Defender*, July 31, 1943.

106. Paul T. Gilbert and J. M. Klein, *Some Light of Truth on the Negro Housing Nightmare* (Chicago: *Chicago Sun*, 1945), 9.

107. *Defender*, December 27, 1941, January 2, 31, February 7, 1942. The best book on the black press is Lee Finkle, *Forum for Protest: The Black Press During World War II* (Rutherford N.J.: Fairleigh Dickinson University Press, 1975).

108. Quoted in Drake and Cayton, *Black Metropolis*, 91–92.

109. *Defender*, July 10, 17, 24, 1943.

110. Cayton and Drake, *Black Metropolis*, 92–93; Homer A. Jack, "Documented Memorandum XIII: The Mayor's Commission on Human Relations," mimeo, CHS Library, 1–2; *Human Relations in Chicago* (Chicago: Mayor's Committee on Race Relations, 1945), passim.

111. *Daily News,* Feb. 4, 1943. Hayakawa later became a columnist for the *Defender* and gained national prominence as head of San Francisco State University during the student antiwar protests of the late 1960s.

112. *Daily News,* Dec. 19, 1941, Feb. 18, 1943.

113. *Daily News,* Dec. 7, 1942; see also letter to the editor, *Tribune*, Aug. 8, 1944.

114. *Daily News,* Feb. 3, May 25, 1944; *Tribune,* July 16, 1944.

115. Quote from *Daily News,* Feb. 3, 1944; Masako M. Osako, "Japanese-Americans: Melting into the All-American Pot," in Melvin Holli and Peter d'A. Jones, *Ethnic Chicago*, 2nd ed. (Grand Rapids, Mich.: Eerdmans, 1984), 526–28; *People in Motion: The Postwar Adjustment of Evacuated Japanese Americans* (Washington, D.C.: U.S. Department of the Interior, War Agency Liquidation Unit, 1947), 145–57.

116. *Poston Chronicle*, May 23, 1943, quoted in Valerie Matsumoto, "Japanese American Women During World War II," in Ellen Carol DuBois and Vicki Ruiz, *Unequal Sisters: A Multicultural Reader in U.S. Women's History* (New York: Routledge, 1990), 383.

117. *People in Motion*, 146, 150–51.

118. Dan Kuzuhara, "Chicago's Resettlers of the 1940s," in Japanese American Citizens League, *29th Biennial National Convention*, 1986, 30–33; Chicago Resettlers Committee, "Progress Report, December 1947," 2.

119. Quote of James Ford, president of the Chicago Real Estate Board, in *Economist* 112 (July 29, 1944):1.

The Production War

1. *Tribune*, June 16, 17, Dec. 16, 1944.

2. *Tribune*, July 10, 25, 1944, Jan. 2, 25, 1945.

3. The district included the northern parts of Illinois and Indiana, as well as Wisconsin, Iowa, Minnesota, North Dakota, and South Dakota. *Tribune*, May 11, 1942.

4. *Commerce* 34 (March 1946):41.

5. Donald Nelson, *Arsenal of Democracy: The Story of American War Production* (New York: Harcourt, Brace, 1946), tells the story in great detail.

6. Chicago Roller Skate Company, Radio Steel and Manufacturing Co., and Vaughn Novelty Company, typescript histories of wartime activities, Illinois War Council Papers, hereafter cited with company name and "wartime history." These are part of a series of histories of homefront activities collected by the Illinois State Library in 1946–47. *Tribune*, June 21, 1944.

7. Ekco, wartime history.

8. *Tribune*, March 25, 1942.

9. *Tribune*, Feb. 20, 1942.

10. Early in 1941, for instance, Western Electric surveyed 1,250 potential subcontractors and distributed contracts to 215 of them. Similarly, construction of the giant Douglas C-54 transport plane on the Northwest Side involved three hundred Chicago subcontractors. One of them, Pullman-Standard, had for two years been building tail sections that were shipped to Long Beach, California, for C-47s. And 50 percent of Link-Belt production came from subcontractors who went through the company's special training facility. *Daily News*, Dec. 2, 1941; *Microphone* 18 (Jan. 1943):1; *Airview News* 1 (July 6, 1943):1; *Airview News* 1 (July 13, 1943):1; *Business Week*, Aug. 15, 1942, 62–63.

11. *Tribune*, March 27, 1942, Dec. 23, 1944; *Daily News*, June 25, 1942; *Business Week*, July 26, 1941, 17; *Business Week*, Nov. 1, 1941, 30; *Business Week*, May 9, 1942, 22, 24; *Business Week*, Sept. 12, 1942, 50.

12. Busch, *They Escaped the Hangman*, 263.

13. *Tribune*, Feb. 5, 1942.

14. *Economist* 106 (July 12, 1941):2; Watters, I:6, 118; Watters, II:118; see ads in *Commerce* 39 (March 1942):9, 97; *Tribune*, March 2, 3, 21, 1942.

15. *Industrial and Commercial Background for Planning Chicago* (Chicago: Chicago Plan Commission, 1942)

24–25, 43, 46; Bessie Louise Pierce, "Studies on Chicago Economic History," typescript, Bessie L. Pierce Papers, University of Chicago Library, 24–25.

16. *Daily News,* Jan. 7, 1944.

17. Kraft Foods, wartime history.

18. Swift revived pemmican, a form of dried meat based on an old Native American formula. Swift and rival Wilson both exported tushonka, a mixture of boiled pork cuts, bay leaves, and spices that was a favorite canned dish among Muscovites. In one of the more ingenious factory conversions, Chicago Vitreous Enamel Product Company, a producer of plumbing fixtures, turned its huge drying ovens and blowers to the task of producing dried eggs. Swift & Company, Kraft Foods, Cracker-Jack, wartime histories; *Business Week,* July 11, 1942, 65; *Business Week,* Aug. 15, 1942, 8; Watters, II:109–110, 143; *Tribune,* Feb. 11, May 1, 1942, June 20, Aug. 19, 1944; *Daily News,* June 24, 1942, Oct. 1, 1943, April 7, 1944.

19. Watters, II:107; on Formfit, *Tribune,* June 22, 1944; Poster Products, Bearse, Phoenix Trimming, wartime histories.

20. Watters, II, 86; *Daily News,* March 28, 1943; *Tribune,* July 1, 1944, Feb. 18, 1945.

21. Wycoff Steel Company, wartime history

22. *Daily News,* Jan. 20, 1943.

23. *Business Week,* May 2, 1942; *Daily News,* Aug. 6, 1943.

24. Watters, II:95–96, 146; *Tribune,* May 1, June 6, 1942, June 16, 1944, Jan. 5, 12, 1945; *Daily News,* March 5, 1943; *Business Week,* Sept. 11, 1943, 17; Pressed Steel Car Company, wartime history. Similar skills in heavy metal fabrication brought contracts for minesweepers, tugs, and tankers to the yacht yards of Henry Grebe & Co. across the North Branch of the Chicago River from Riverview Park, while Chicago Bridge and Iron built 157 LSTs and forty-five dry docks at its Seneca plant, seventy-five miles southwest of the city. Henry C. Grebe & Co., wartime history; *Business Week,* March 14, 1942, 19; on Seneca, see Robert J. Havighurst and H. Gerthon Morgan, *The Social History of a War-Boom Community* (New York: Longmans, Green, 1951), a sociological classic.

25. Diamond-T Motor Car Company, Templeton, Kenly & Co, Burgess-Norton Mfg. Co, wartime histories; Forrest Crissey, *American Fighting Power Flows from Geneva, Illinois* (1943); *Economist* 108 (Oct. 24, 1942):2.

26. Watters, II:131; Barber-Greene, Link-Belt, General Motors Electro-Motive Division, the Buda Company, wartime histories; *Tribune,* May 13, 1942, June 12, 1944; *Diesel War Power* (Detroit: General Motors Corporation, 1945), passim, is a colorful history.

27. Verson Allsteel Press Company, United Specialties Company, wartime histories; *Tribune,* June 18, 1944; Helene Curtis, Schwinn, wartime histories.

28. Stewart-Warner, The Seng Company, Borg-Warner, Semler Company, L. A. Young Spring and Wire Corporation, General Engineering Works, Lincoln Manufacturing Co., F. H. Noble and Company, Elgin Watch Company, wartime histories.

29. *Daily News,* June 2, July 6, 1943; *Business Week,* Feb. 27, 1943, 68; see also issues of *Silver Streak,* the Amertorp employee magazine.

30. *Daily News,* Jan. 18, 1944. Besides Wurlitzer in DeKalb, there was the Howard Aircraft Company, located next to the Geneva Airport. It produced small air ambulances and trainers, and on Jan. 18, 1944, it celebrated the completion of its seven-hundredth plane.

31. *Tribune,* Feb. 14, 26, March 22, 26, June 6, 1942.

32. *Daily News,* June 18, 1942.

33. Walmark Mfg. Co., Aurora Metal Company, Kropp Forge Co., wartime histories; Watters, II:75.

34. *Commerce* 38 (Feb. 1941):29, 40; Studebaker Corporation, wartime history; *Daily News,* May 15, 1943; *Tribune,* Feb. 9, 1942, June 17, Aug. 30, 1944.

35. *Daily News,* June 17, 1942, March 17, 1944; *Tribune,* March 19, May 20, June 7, 1942, Nov. 8, 1944, Feb. 9, 1945; Terry B. Dunham and Lawrence R. Gustin, *The Buick: A Complete History,* 3rd ed., (Myomissing, Penn: Automobile Quarterly, 1987).

36. *Daily News,* June 3, 4, 1942, March 27, 1943, June 13, 1944; *Tribune,* Feb. 19, June 4, 7, 1942, June 13, Dec. 15, 1944, March 24, 1945; *Economist* 107 (Feb. 21, 1942):1; *Economist* 107 (May 2, 1942):1; *Business Week,* Aug. 28, 1941, 82.

37. *Tribune,* June 10, 1942; *Economist* 108 (Aug. 8, 1942):1, 8; *Daily News,* Feb. 12, 23, 1943.

38. *Daily News,* March 31, 1943; *Airview News* 1 (June 8, 1943):1.

39. *Daily News,* July 31, 1943; *Airview News* 1 (July 20, 1943):8; *Airview News* 1 (Aug. 3, 1943):2, 5.

40. *Airview News* 1 (Aug. 3, 1943):1.

41. C. Clare & Co., Powers Regulator Company, Minneapolis–Honeywell Regulator Company, wartime histories; *Powers News*, April 1944, passim; *Powers News*, summer 1944, passim; on the auto pilot, *Daily News*, Sept. 21, 1943; *Tribune*, June 13, July 3, 10, 1944.

42. Watters, II, 104; *Tribune*, Feb. 16, March 23, 1942; *Daily News*, Jan. 27, 1944.

43. Shure Brothers, Inc., Galvin Manufacturing Corporation, Western Electric Company, Zenith Radio Corporation, wartime histories.

44. *Tribune*, Sept. 21, 1944.

45. *Tribune*, July 25, Aug. 27, Sept. 2, 11, 1944; *Daily News*, Jan. 27, 28, 1944.

46. *Microphone* 16 (June 1941):1; *Economist* 107 (Feb. 7, 1942):3; *Economist* 108 (Oct. 17, 1942):28.

47. *Commerce* 39 (June 1942):9.

48. *Tribune*, May 1, June 5, 1942, July 5, 1944; Diamond Wire & Cable Co., wartime history.

49. *Tribune*, June 16, 1944; H. M. Harper Company, wartime history.

50. Mills Industries, The Rudolph Wurlitzer Company, Santay Corporation, Albert Zollinger, Inc., wartime histories; *Microphone* 18 (Nov. 1942):6.

51. *Tribune*, June 7, 1942.

52. Abbott Laboratories, wartime history; *Daily News*, Nov. 10, 1943; *Tribune*, Jan. 20, 1945.

53. *Tribune*, Jan. 19, 1945.

54. James Baxter, *Scientists Against Time* (Boston: Little, Brown, 1946), 419–33.

55. The best brief summary of events is *The First Reactor* (Washington, D.C.: U.S. Department of Energy, 1982).

56. Thomas J. Crawford, "Participation of the Chicago Public Schools in the War Effort" (Unpublished master's thesis, DePaul University, 1946), 53–60; William H. Johnson, "Industrial Education in the War Program," *School and Society* 55 (May 30, 1942): 597–600.

57. Watters, I:367; *Tribune* Jan. 1, 4, 1942; *War Production Training in the Chicago Public Schools* (Chicago: Board of Education, n.d.), 1–2.

58. Watters, I:111–12; Watters, II:69; *Microphone* 7 (Aug. 1941):3; *Microphone* 7 (Oct. 1941):3; *Airview News* 1 (June 22, 1943):3, 6; *Airview News* 1 (Nov. 16, 1943):16; *Daily News*, April 15, 1943.

59. *Tribune*, Jan. 21, 25, Feb. 2, March 15, 19, 24, 1942, June 6, 17, 1944.

60. Admissions were selective, generating some resentment among unsuccessful applicants. *Tribune*, March 4, 10, 15, 24, June 7, 1942, June 20, 24, Aug. 15, 1944, May 23, 1945; see especially the sketch of IIT president Harold Heald, *Daily News*, Jan. 18, 1944.

61. *Daily News*, Jan. 9, Nov. 26, 1943, Feb. 24, March 20, 1944; *Tribune*, June 12, 1942, June 25, 1944; Watters, I:245.

62. *Tribune*, July 9, 1944; *Airview News*, 1 (June 15, 1943):3.

63. *Tribune*, June 13, 1943, Dec. 4, 1943; *Daily News*, Oct. 21, 1943; *Economist* 108 (Dec. 15, 1942):28; Watters, II:252; *Airview News* 1 (Aug. 10, 1943):5.

64. *Tribune*, May 12, 24, 25, 31, June 2, 1942, July 8, 15, 28, Sept. 10, 1944; *Daily News*, June 20, 1942, March 22, June 9, July 1, 1943; Illinois State Council of Defense, Meeting Minutes, April 12, 1943, Illinois War Council Papers, 13.

65. *Daily News*, June 22, 1943, Feb. 21, 1944.

66. Louise Kerr, "Mexican Chicago: Chicano Pluralism Aborted, 1939–1954," in Holli and Jones, *Ethnic Chicago*, 272–80.

67. *Sun*, May 22, 1943; Watters, II:273; *Daily News*, Oct. 22, 23, Nov. 8, 1943.

68. John Hope Franklin, *From Slavery to Freedom: A History of Negro Americans*, 3rd ed. (New York: Knopf, 1967), 576–80. See also the local FEPC files for Region VI, record group 228, National Archives and Records Service, Chicago Branch. Box 89 has an excellent record of a prolonged controversy over employment at the Chicago Studebaker plant. See also "Special Report on Negro Labor in Chicago," Feb. 10, 1943, in Chicago files, record group 44, boxes 1939–40, OWI files.

69. Watters, I:406; Watters, II:235, 261–65, 273, 277–78; *Sun*, May 22, 1943.

70. The Chicago team, the Colleens, played at Stewbridge Park on the South Side, but a change in venue often brought them to a military base or hospital. The league first played underhand twelve-inch softball, but over its twelve-year existence it evolved into overhand hardball. *Tribune*, July 12, 1982; *Wall Street Journal*, July 8, 1988. See also Susan M. Cahn, "No Freaks, No Amazons, No Boyish Bobs," *Chicago History* 18 (Spring 1989):26–41.

71. Quote, *Daily News*, Nov. 19, 1943; elevator operators, *Economist* 106

(Oct. 18, 1941):34; streetcars, *Tribune*, Jan. 17, 1945; on Illinois Central, *Daily News*, April 24, 1943.

72. Quote, Daily News, April 19, 1943; navy convoy, *Daily News*, Sept. 16–18, 1943; mail trucks, *Tribune*, Dec. 16, 1944; Watters, II:174–75, 253. Virginia MacLean is pictured in *Business Week*, Dec. 12, 1942, 10.

73. On police, *Daily News*, Sept. 21, Oct. 10, 1943; *Tribune*, Feb. 16, May 17, 1942; *American City* 58 (Sept. 1943): 64; on lifeguards, *American City* 58 (Sept. 1943):65; *Daily News*, April 7, June 23, 1943; *Tribune*, July 23, 1944; on bouncer and bartender, *Tribune*, Jan. 10, 1945; *Daily News*, Sept. 21, 1943.

74. *Tribune*, March 25, June 5, 1942, Nov. 25, 1944, Feb. 14, 1945; *Daily News*, June 21, Oct. 1, 1943.

75. Men dominated the secretarial field earlier because the bold handwriting they were taught was regarded as properly forceful in business correspondence, while female penmanship was meant to be delicate and nondemanding. The typewriter concealed the gender of its user, thus allowing office managers to hire lower-paid female secretaries. *Daily News*, June 15, 1943.

76. For instance, women constituted nearly 50 percent of the work force of the mammoth Western Electric Hawthorne Works, 60 percent at Galvin, Wells–Gardner, and Webster–Chicago, 70 percent at Continental, and 80 percent at Shure Brothers, Guthman, and Bendix Aviation. "Nimble fingers" quote from *Microphone* 18 (Oct. 1942):1; *Tribune*, Feb. 13, 1942, June 7, 1944; figures for indi-

vidual companies tallied from figures submitted to Illinois State Historical Library's war history project in wartime histories, Illinois War Council Papers.

77. *Daily News*, May 24, 1943; *Tribune*, June 14, 1944; *Airview News* 1 (July 13, 1943):3; *Airview News* 1 (Aug. 24, 1943):5.

78. First quote, *Daily News*, Jan. 20, 1943; second quote, letter to the editor, *Daily News*, April 3, 1943.

79. *Daily News*, Jan. 20, 1943.

80. On Elwood, *Daily News*, April 28, 1943; Watters, II:254; on one blast, which killed five women at the Lion Manufacturing Company, see *Daily News*, Jan. 26, 1944.

81. *Tribune*, Feb. 24, 1942.

82. *Microphone* 17 (Dec. 1941):5; *Airview News* 1 (June 22, 1943):3; on Commonwealth–Edison security, *Daily News*, June 18, 1942; *CDA* 1 (July 7, 1942):4; on Carnegie Steel, *CDA* 2 (Aug. 1943):3.

83. See especially Ralph H. Burke notebook, miscellaneous collection, OCD Papers. Burke was in charge of the Protective Service of the Chicago civilian defense district; *Digest in Question and Answer for Protection of Industry Based on Industrial Conference* (Chicago: Office of Civilian Defense, April 1942); Worner quote, *CDA* 1 (May 1942):46.

84. *Airview News* 1 (July 6, 1943):1; *Airview News* 1 (Oct. 26, 1943):5.

85. *Daily News*, March 4, June 3, 1943; Watters, II:291–92, 294.

86. *Daily News*, June 5–7, 26, 1942; *Tribune*, June 6–7, 1942.

87. *Airview News* 1 (Jan. 4, 1944):3; Watters, II:291; *Daily News*, Nov. 2,

1943; *Tribune* Jan. 8, 1945; *Microphone*, 18 (Sept. 1942):2.

88. *Airview News*, 1 (June 15, 1943):7.

89. Watters, I:337; *Tribune*, March 13, 14, 21, June 6, 1942; *Daily News*, Jan. 15, 1943.

90. *Microphone* 18 (Jan. 1943):5; *Microphone* 18 (Nov. 1942):2; *CDA* 2 (Jan. 6, 1943):1, 4; *Economist* 110 (Oct. 2, 1943):1; *Airview News* 1 (July 6, 1943):8.

91. Watters, II:76–78.

92. War Department press release, Dec. 5, 1945, Army–Navy "E" files, Illinois War Council Papers, i–ii, 11–18.

93. Watters, II:295, 331.

94. Watters, II:331; *Tribune*, March 20, 1942, June 17, 1944; *Daily News*, Feb. 1, 3, 5, 1943.

95. John F. Zwicky, "A State at War: The Home Front in Illinois During the Second World War" (Unpublished Ph.D. diss., Loyola University, 1989), includes an able summary of the complex Ward issue.

The Crossroads City

1. *Daily News*, Feb. 16–18, 25, March 27, 29, April 13, 1943; on the construction and dedication of the replacement USS *Chicago*, which was commissioned on Jan. 10, 1945, see *Daily News*, June 3, 1944; *Tribune*, Aug. 11, 21, 1944, Jan. 10, March 29, 1945.

2. "Chicago Police Adding to Police Motorcycle Force," *American City* 56 (Jan. 1941):49, 75; "Handling Special Events," *American City* 56 (Nov. 1941):83, 85, 87.

3. *Daily News*, June 14, 24, 1942, July 2, 1943; *CDA* 2 (June 1943):8.

4. *Daily News*, June 8, 11, 1942; *Tribune*, June 8, 1942.

5. *Daily News,* May 21, 1943.

6. *Daily News,* Jan. 4, Sept. 24, 1943, Jan. 3, 1944; *CDA* 2 (Oct. 22, 1943):3.

7. *Tribune*, Dec. 23, 1944.

8. *Tribune*, Dec. 10, 1944.

9. *Daily News,* Aug. 25, 1943.

10. *Tribune*, June 12, 1944.

11. *Daily News,* Aug. 28, 1943.

12. *Tribune*, May 9, 1942.

13. *Daily News,* June 16, 1943.

14. *Tribune*, May 3, 7, 1942.

15. *Tribune*, June 13, 1942.

16. *Tribune*, June 7, 1944.

17. *Tribune*, Nov. 17, 18, 1944; *Sun*, Oct. 10, 1943.

18. *Sun*, June 6, 7, 1943.

19. *CDA* 2 (April 7, 1943):1; *CDA* 2 (Aug. 1943):1; *CDA* 2 (Sept. 10, 1943):1; *Daily News*, April 8, 10, 13–16, Sept. 16, 21, 22, 28–30, Oct. 9, Nov. 10, 11, 1943, Jan. 11, 18, Feb. 1, 1944; *Sun*, Aug. 28, 1943; *Tribune*, Sept. 9, 1943, June 10, 25, July 9, 16, Aug. 8, Nov. 20, 1944; *Economist* 108 (Sept. 26, 1943):29.

20. *Daily News,* Sept. 20, 1943, June 18, 1944.

21. *Tribune*, June 5, 1944.

22. *Daily News,* Jan. 27, Feb. 9, 1944.

23. The radio listings in the daily newspapers contain hundreds of notices about special war programs. On radio concentration, see *Tribune*, Feb. 4, 1945.

24. *Tribune*, June 7, 1942, Jan. 6, 14, Feb. 11, 1945; *Daily News*, June 5, 1944.

25. Headline, *Daily News*, Dec. 19, 1941; see also *Daily News*, Dec. 20, 1941, and *Tribune*, Jan. 3, 1942.

26. *Daily News,* June 15, 1942, April 5, 29, 1943; *Tribune*, Feb. 1, March 13, 26, May 2, 30, 1942, June 4, 1944; *Sun*, July 15, 1942; *Economist* 107 (May 9, 1942):8; *Economist* 107 (June 27, 1942):8; *Economist* 108 (Dec. 12, 1942):8; *Economist* 109 (Jan. 2, 1943):8; *Economist* 110 (Oct. 23, 1943):8.

27. Quotes, *Tribune*, June 7, 1942, and *Business Week*, Dec. 4, 1943; *Tribune*, March 19, 21, May 10, 1942; *Daily News*, June 12, 20, 1942.

28. Watters, I:129–30; *Daily News,* Oct. 1, 1943.

29. Watters, I:131; *Tribune*, Jan. 1, 1942; *Daily News*, June 6, 1942.

30. Quote, *Daily News,* March 27, 1943; Watters, II:189; *Tribune*, May 19, June 2, 1942.

31. *Daily News,* June 2, 1943; *Tribune*, March 14, May 19, June 5, 1942, Nov. 26, 1944.

32. *War Production Training in the Chicago Public Schools,* 2.

33. On universities and the war, see Watters, I:133–35.

34. *Tribune*, March 19, 1942, Feb. 7, 1945; *Daily News,* Feb. 12, 1944.

35. *Tribune*, July 12, 1942, Sept. 10, 1944; *Daily News,* March 26, 1943.

36. *Tribune*, Jan. 30, June 12, 1942, Jan. 14, 27, 1945; *CDA* 1 (June 16, 1942):6; *Daily News*, June 1, 1942, March 2, 1943; on the yacht fleet, see *Tribune*, June 7, 1942, *Daily News*, May 8, 1944.

37. *Tribune*, Oct. 27, 1946.

38. Watters, I:136–37; *Tribune*, May 7–10, 15, 24, 1942; *Business Week*, July 18, 1942, 17; *Business Week*, Sept. 5, 1942, 17–18; *Business Week*, Feb. 27, 1943, 70; *Business Week*, July 10, 1943, 28, 30, 32; *Business Week*, Aug. 7, 1943, 81; *Business Week*, Sept. 18, 1943, 32, 34; *Business Week*, Oct. 23, 1943, 20; *Daily News,* Jan. 9, Feb. 3, 11, April 30, June 15, 19, Aug. 10, Sept. 2, 4, 9, 21, 1943, Jan. 10, 1944; *Economist* 110 (July 24, 1943):1; *Economist* 110 (Aug. 7, 1943):9; *Economist* 110 (Sept. 11, 1943):1.

39. *Daily News,* April 8, 1943.

40. *Tribune*, Nov. 20, 1944; *Daily News,* Dec. 18, 1941, June 4, 1942, April 8, 1943; *Economist* 108 (Sept. 26, 1942):2; *Economist* 108 (Dec. 19, 1942):8; *Economist* 108 (Dec. 26, 1942):8; *Economist* 109 (June 26, 1943):8; *Economist* 111 (March 4, 1944):3.

41. *Tribune*, March 8, 1942, Feb. 18, 1945.

42. *Daily News,* March 3, 1943.

43. *Daily News,* Nov. 1, 1943.

44. *Tribune*, Nov. 30, 1942.

45. *Daily News,* June 23, 1942, June 4, Sept. 16, Oct. 15, 1943.

46. Robert M. Yoder, "Chicago Throws A Party," *Saturday Evening Post*, July 18, 1942, 22–23, 62–63.

47. *Times*, Sept. 5, 1941.

48. *Sun*, Aug. 13, 1946.

49. *Tribune*, Jan. 14, March 1, 4, 8, June 7, 1942, July 2, 25, Sept. 12, 1944; *Daily News*, June 5, 22, 1942, Feb. 17, March 31, April 1, 10, 27, July 6, 7, Sept. 16, Nov. 3, 1943, Jan. 22, Feb. 14, 1944.

50. Quote, *Daily News,* June 22, 1942; *CDA* 2 (Dec. 9, 1942):6; *CDA* 2 (June 25, 1943):1; *CDA* 2 (Aug. 27, 1943):1; "History of the USO of Illinois, Inc., and Predecessor Organ-

izations, 1941–1991" (typescript, United Service Organizations of Illinois, Inc., 1991), 6.

51. *CDA* 1 (Dec. 2, 1942):3; *CDA* 2 (June 25, 1943):1; *CDA* 2 (July 9, 1943):1; *Daily News,* Feb. 17, April 10, 1943.

52. Quote, *CDA* 2 (Dec. 9, 1942):6; "History of the USO," 6–9; on other USO activities, see *Tribune*, May 26, June 4–6, 1942, July 28, Aug. 27, Oct. 12, 1944; *Daily News,* Jan. 18, March 16, 22, July 22, 1943, Feb. 8, 1944; on other organizations, see *Daily News,* Jan. 9, 22, 1943, Jan. 13, 17, 1944; *Tribune*, June 6, 1942, Dec. 10, 1944; Watters, I:162.

53. *CDA* 2 (March 24, 1943):3. The writer of a *Tribune* article, June 28, 1943, was apparently unaware of the AWVS lounge.

Inventing the Postwar World

1. Quote, *Daily News*, August 15, 1945; see also *Daily News*, August 13, 1945, for precelebration plans and August 14, 16, 1945, for additional stories. The *Tribune* and *Sun* are similarly filled with celebration stories.

2. *Daily News*, August 16, 1945.

3. *Daily News*, August 11, 1945.

4. *Daily News*, *Tribune*, August 14–25, 1945.

5. *Daily News*, *Tribune*, August 14–25, 1945.

6. *Daily News*, February 7, April 7, 1944, August 18, 1945.

7. There is an illustrated article in *Tribune*, January 21, 1945. See also the perceptive series by Tom Collins in *Daily News*, September 21, 24, 1943.

8. *Daily News*, August 17, 1945.

9. Jerry Flint, The Dream Machine: *The Golden Age of American Automobiles, 1946–1965* (New York: Quadrangle,1976)1–58.

10. *Commerce* 43 (March 1946):41–42.

11. Larry Wolters, "Electronics: A $5 Billion Industry Born in Chicago," *The Chicago Story* (Chicago: Chicago Association of Commerce and Industry, 1954), 62–64, 292, 294.

12. Final state approval for the Congress Street Expressway (now the Eisenhower) came in December 1943. On suburban trends, see *Daily News*, September 21–23, 1943; *Economist* 112 (December 16, 1944):1, 9.

13. William H. Whyte, *The Organization Man* (New York: Simon and Schuster, 1956) is the classic study.

14. Many articles were written on airport site selection between 1943 and 1945, but see especially, *Tribune*, March 13–22, 1945.

15. *Tribune*, November 16, 19, 1944; *Daily News*, September 18, 29, October 1, 4, 1943.

16. *Sun*, November 14, 21, 1945.

17. Perry R. Duis, "Yesterday's City: Butch O'Hare, Chicago's Borrowed Hero," *Chicago History* 17 (Fall/Winter 1988–89):102–110.

18. *Tribune*, July 9, August 12, 1944; *Daily News*, August 26, 1943, April 20, 1944.

19. Watters, II:281–85; *Human Relations in Chicago* (Chicago: Mayor's Committee on Race Relations, 1945) is a good summary of the status of race relations in the fall of 1945.

20. Watters, I:433–34.

21. *Daily News*, May 21, 22, June 2, 1943, May 4, November 12, 1944, March 22, 1945.

Chronology of World War II

1939

September 1   Germany invades Poland; World War II begins

November 3   Congress passes "cash and carry" amendment to Neutrality Laws

1940

May 14   Netherlands surrenders

May 26   Allied evacuation at Dunkirk (to June 4)

May 28   Belgium capitulates to Germans

June 9   Norway surrenders

June 10   Italy enters the war

June 22   France signs armistice with Germany

August 27   U.S. draft law enacted

September 16   Mobilization of U.S. National Guard begins (through Oct. 1941)

November 5   Roosevelt elected for third term

1941

March 11   U.S. Lend-Lease Act signed

April 13   U.S.S.R. and Japan sign Neutrality Pact

June 22   Germany invades USSR

August 9   Roosevelt and Churchill meet in Atlantic Conference; Atlantic Charter proclaimed

December 7   Pacific war begins with Japanese attacks on U.S. and British posts (Pearl Harbor and Malaya)

December 8   United States declares war on Japan

December 11   Germany and Italy declare war on U.S.

1942

February 22   Roosevelt orders MacArthur to leave Philippines

April 18   U.S. (Doolittle) B-25 raid on Japanese

May 4   Battle of the Coral Sea (to May 8)

June 3   Battle of Midway (to June 6)

August 7   U.S. Marines and Army land on Guadalcanal

August 17   U.S. Eighth Air Force makes first attack on European target (Rouen-Sotteville)

September 15   U.S. Army lands in New Guinea

1943

January 14   Allied Casablanca Conference begins (to Jan. 23)

February 9   U.S. forces complete Guadalcanal campaign

March 16	Convoy battle is climax of Battle of the Atlantic (to March 20)
April 19	Jewish uprising in Warsaw ghetto
June 21	U.S. forces land on New Georgia
July 10	Allies invade Sicily
September 8	Eisenhower announces Italian surrender
October 14	U.S. B-17s suffer heavy losses in raid on Schweinfurt
November 1	U.S. Marines land on Bouganville

1944

January 16	Eisenhower assumes duties as Supreme Commander, Allied Expeditionary Force
January 22	U.S. Army lands at Anzio
February 17	U.S. forces land on Eniwetok atoll
May 23	U.S. Army breaks out at Anzio beachhead
June 6	Allies land at Normandy (Operation Overlord)
June 15	U.S. Marines and Army invade Saipan
June 19	Battle of the Philippine Sea (to June 20)
July 21	U.S. Marines and Army land on Guam
July 24	U.S. Marines land on Tinian
August 1	Warsaw Uprising begins
August 9	Eisenhower establishes headquarters in France
August 25	Paris liberated
October 23	Battle for Leyte Gulf (to October 26)

November 7	Roosevelt elected to fourth term
November 24	United States begins B-29 raids on Japan
December 16	Germans attack in Ardennes (Battle of the Bulge)

1945

January 9	U.S. Army lands on Luzon
February 4	Yalta Conference begins (to Feb. 12)
February 19	U.S. Marines land on Iwo Jima
March 7	U.S. Army crosses Rhine on bridge at Remagen
April 1	U.S. forces land on Okinawa
April 12	Roosevelt dies; Truman succeeds.
April 25	United Nations conference opens in San Francisco
April 28	Mussolini is executed
April 30	Hitler dies in bunker
May 7	All German forces surrender unconditionally
May 8	Proclaimed V-E Day
July 16	Big Three begin Potsdam Conference (to Aug. 2)
July 16	Atomic bomb successfully tested at Los Alamos
August 6	Atomic bomb dropped on Hiroshima
August 9	Atomic bomb dropped on Nagasaki
August 14	Japan surrenders, ending World War II

Bibliographic Essay

The literature on World War II, like that in many fields of American history, is uneven. Scholars have pored over some areas with great care; other topics have barely been tapped. One such gap has been the impact of the war on everyday life in the largest American cities. Chicago is a good place to start.

This catalogue benefited from several rich primary sources. The Illinois War Council records, housed at the Illinois State Archives in Springfield, were the most important. The collection originated shortly after the war, when the Illinois State Historical Library hired Mary Watters to compile a history of the state homefront. The first result of this effort is the magnificently detailed and documented *Illinois During the Second World War* (2 vols., Springfield: Illinois State Historical Library, 1951–52). The second is a mountain of in-formation, although the Chicago coverage is sparse. The documentation of corporate activities is particularly rich. The Chicago Historical Society Library holds a smaller quantity of similar material.

Several local manuscript collections, most notably the Travellers' Aid Society Collection at the University of Illinois at Chicago and the records of the Haupt trials at the National Archives–Chicago Branch, were also important resources. The papers of sociologists Ernest Burgess and Louis Wirth served well as a guide to journal literature.

Two unpublished theses were also valuable. John F. Zwicky, "A State at War: The Home Front in Illinois During the Second World War" (Ph.D. diss., Loyola University of Chicago, 1989) concentrates on economic and political activities. Annabelle Bender, "Civilian Defense Block Organization in Hyde Park," (Master's thesis, The University of Chicago, 1943) is a good contemporary view.

The literature on Chicago during the war is especially spotty. Roger Biles, *Big City Boss in Depression and War* (DeKalb: Northern Illinois University Press, 1984) spends too little time on Mayor Edward J. Kelly's war leadership. James C. Schneider, *Should America Go To War? The Debate over Foreign Policy in Chicago, 1939–1941* (Chapel Hill: University of North Carolina Press, 1989) offers a detailed account of the isolation vs. intervention debate. Works on Chicago's black community include St. Clair Drake and Horace Cayton's magnificently detailed *Black Metropolis* (New York: Harcourt, Brace, 1945) and Arnold Hirsch, *Making the Second Ghetto: Race and Housing in Chicago, 1940–1960* (New York: Cambridge University Press, 1983). Aside from oral histories, which substitute immediacy for breadth of coverage, the rich detail of the daily press remains the single most important source for the history of Chicago's homefront.

The national literature on the homefront is mixed. Richard Polenberg, *War and Society: The United States, 1941–1945* (Westport, Conn.: Greenwood Press, 1972) and his documentary collection *America At War: The Home Front, 1941–1945* (Englewood Cliffs, N.J.: Prentice Hall, 1968) focus on the government rather than everyday life. The same is true of John Morton Blum, *V Was for Victory: Poli-*

tics and American Culture During World War II (New York: Harcourt, Brace, 1976). Everyday life is best treated in John Costello, *Virtue Under Fire: How World War II Changed Our Social and Sexual Attitudes* (Boston: Little, Brown, 1985). Studs Terkel, *The Good War: An Oral History of World War II* (New York: Pantheon, 1984) and a special oral history symposium in *Journal of American History 77* (September 1990) represent the best of that type of source. The richest social history is Richard Lingemann, *Don't You Know There's a War On? The American Home Front, 1941–1945* (New York: G.P. Putnan, 1970). Mark H. Leff, "The Politics of Sacrifice on the American Home Front in World War II," *Journal of American History 77* (March 1991):1296–1318 is also valuable.

The literature on urban America during World War II is just beginning to appear. Philip J. Funigiello, *The Challenge to Urban Liberalism: Federal-City Relations During World War II* (Knoxville: University of Tennessee Press, 1978) is an excellent account of the struggle over whether the war should become a domestic reform crusade. The chronological organization of Betty Burnett, *St. Louis at War: The Story of a City, 1941–1945* (St. Louis: Patrice Press, 1987) makes it a practical source, while several valuable articles may be found in Roger W. Lotchin, *The Martial Metropolis: U.S. Cities in War and Peace* (Westport, Conn.: Greenwood Press, 1984).

The richest literature is about women during the war. Sherna Berger Gluck, *Rosie the Riveter Revisited: Women, the War, and Social Change* (Boston: G.K. Hall, 1987) is based on oral histories. Maureen Honey, *Creating Rosie the Riveter: Class, Gender, and Propaganda During World War II* (Amherst: University of Massachusetts Press, 1984) makes imaginative use of popular fiction. Susan Hartmann, *The Homefront and Beyond: American Women in*

the 1940s (Boston: G.K. Hall, 1982) is especially useful because of its decade-long perspective. D'Ann Campbell, *Women at War With America: Private Lives in a Patriotic Era* (Cambridge, Mass.: Harvard University Press, 1984) concentrates on family structure, while Doris Weatherford, *American Women and World War II* (New York: Facts on File, 1990) provides the most complete treatment of women in the military, as well as the workplace and the home.

Finally, Paul Boyer, *By the Bomb's Early Light: American Thought and Culture at the Dawn of the Atomic Age* (New York: Pantheon, 1985) captures superbly the mixture of pride, fear, and confusion that emerged at the end of the war. James P. Baxter II, *Scientists Against Time* (Boston: Little, Brown, 1946) explores how technology and medical research won the war.

Illustration Credits

Introduction

x left top and middle, James Norton; x left bottom, CHS Prints and Photographs Collection; x right, CHS, DNA-9513; 2 above left, Fight for Freedom Archives, Princeton University Library; 2 above right, CHS, ICHi-21468; 2 below, America First Committee Collection, Hoover Institution Archives, Stanford University; 3, Mr. and Mrs. Walter Krutz.

The Household War

4, service flag, CHS Decorative and Industrial Arts Collection; 4, window card, CHS Prints and Photographs Collection; 4, "Axe the Axis" pin, two-star service pin, and "Sweetheart Serving U.S. Army" pin, James Norton; 5 above, James Norton; 5 below, CHS Decorative and Industrial Arts Collection; 6 above, Idair and Ronald Taradash; 6 below, CHS Prints and Photographs Collection; 7 above, Ted and Eleanor Ringman; 7 middle, Gerald L. Walsdorf; 7 below, CHS Prints and Photographs Collection; 8 above, CHS Prints and Photographs Collection; 8 below, Schwinn History Center; 9, victory pins, James Norton; 9 below, Royna Rogers Johnson; 10 above, Russell Lewis and Mary Jane Jacob; 10 below, Doreen Hedberg; 11, Ray Martinez; 12, Marie Bruck Molk; 13 above right, Mrs. Irving Rosenbaum; 13 middle right, Mrs. Henry Buchbinder; 13 below, Bob Van Pelt; 14, James Norton; 15 above, James Norton; 15 below, Chicago Public Library; 16 left, Betty J. Rossbach; 16 right, Susan and Thomas Gamnes; 17 above, Lillian Janus; 17 below, Susan and Thomas Gamnes; 18 above right, Evanston Historical Society; 18 below left, from the *Chicago Herald-American*, Mr. and Mrs. Edward Lace; 19 above, *Chicago Sun-Times* Inc.; 19 below, Dr. Ann Englander; 20, Cathy L. Rocca; 22 above, CHS Prints and Photographs Collection; 22 below, John Kowalik; 23, CHS Library; 24 above, Chicago Public Library; 24 below, Leonard Impastato; 25, Mr. and Mrs. John Vanlier; 26 above, James Norton; 26 below, Paul Adler; 27, National Archives; 28 above and below, CHS Prints and Photographs Collection; 29, CHS Prints and Photographs Collection; 30 right, Susan and Thomas Gamnes; 31, Idair and Ronald Taradash.

The Neighborhood War

32, sack, Historical Museum of Addison; 32, yarmulke, Spertus Museum of Judaica; 32, CD banner, Mr. and Mrs. Walter Krutz; 32, telegram, Stewart Pearce; 32, photograph, Joseph Lengyel Square, Mr. and Mrs. Walter Krutz; 33 above, "Vicki Victory" detail from a hairpin package, Florence Krueger; 33 below, James Norton; 34 left, detail from photograph, CHS Prints and Photographs Collection; 34 right, detail from photograph, Barbara Hrdina; 35 above, CHS Prints and Photographs Collection; 35 below, detail from photograph, CHS Prints and Photograph Collection; 36 above, CHS Prints and Photographs Collection; 36 below, Bernice Narbut Kaufmann; 37 above, CHS Prints and Photographs Collection; 37 below John Halvorsen and Richard Halvorsen in memory of Soren and Esther Halvorsen; 38 left, John Halvorsen and Richard Halvorsen in memory of Soren and Esther Halvorsen; 38 right, Sylvia Hornstein in memory of Henry H. Hornstein; 39, Henry Sharton; 40, CHS Prints and Photographs Collection; 41 above, CHS Prints and Photographs Collection; 41 below, Mr. and Mrs. Walter Krutz; 42 above, John Kowalik; 42 below, Mr. and Mrs. Walter Krutz; 43, CHS Prints and Photographs Collection; 44 above, John Kowalik; 44 below, The University of Illinois at Chicago; 45, CHS Library; 46 above, Kraft General Foods, Inc.; 46 below, CHS Prints and Photographs Collection; 47, Elmhurst Historical Museum; 48 below and inset, CHS Prints and Photographs Collection; 49 above and below, CHS Prints and Photographs Collection; 50 below, CHS Prints and Photographs Collection; 51 above, Todd Stump; 51 below, Chicago Jewish Archives; 52, James Norton; 53, The DuSable Museum of African American History, Inc.; 54 above, CHS Prints and Photographs Collection; 54 middle left, James Norton; 54 below right, CHS Prints and Photographs Collection; 56 above, photograph by Dorothea Lange, National Archives; 56 below, The Japanese American

Citizens League; 57 above, The Japanese American Citizens League; 57 below, Navistar International Transportation Corporation; 58, Florence Krueger.

Color Plates

63, CHS Prints and Photographs Collection; 64, CHS Paintings and Sculpture Collection; 65, CHS Library; 66–67 above, Mr. and Mrs. Mitsuo Kodama; 66 below, CHS Prints and Photographs Collection; 67 below, CHS Prints and Photographs Collection; 68, CHS Prints and Photographs Collection; 69, Vargas girls playing cards, Ray Martinez; 69, paper dolls, Doreen Hedburg.

The Production War

66, torpedo, Naval Historical Center; 66, button, "I Am Investing 10% Or More In War Bonds," James Norton; 66, poster, "This Is My Fight Too!", Thomas and Susan Gamnes; 66, poster, C-54 over Chicago, Martin Stanton; 66, button, "Dr. Scholl's/ Member 5th War Bond Drive," James Norton; 67 above, Mrs. John E. Long; 67 below, CHS Prints and Photographs Collection; 68 above, CHS Prints and Photographs Collection; 68 below left and right, James Norton; 69 above, CHS Prints and Photographs Collection; 69 below, advertisement from *Men and Events*, May 1945, CHS Library; 70, Kraft General Foods, Inc.; 71 right, Richard Bitterman; 71 left, Kraft General Foods, Inc.; 72 above, Gail Barazani; 72 below, Hedrich-Blessing Collection, CHS Prints and Photographs Collection; 73, R. Ford Bentley; 74 above, Schwinn History Center; 74 below, CHS Prints and Photographs Collection; 75, McDonnell Douglas; 76 above, Studebaker National Museum; 76 below, Chrysler Corporation; 77, McDonnell Douglas; 78, Shure Brothers, Inc.; 79 above, Zenith Electronics Corporation; 79 below, Steve Bartkowski; 80 middle, disposable blood filters, Les and Ron Kocour; 80, Abbott Laboratories; 81 above, National Archives; 81 below, CHS Paintings and Sculpture Collection; 82 above, Ann Marie McCall in memory of Anna Smiljanic; 82 below, Robert Guritz in memory of Grace King; 83, CHS Prints and Photographs Collection; 84, Library of Congress; 85 above and below, CHS Prints and Photographs Collection; 86, CHS Prints and Photographs Collection; 87, Copyright, *Chicago Tribune* Company, all rights reserved, used with permission; 88, Studebaker National Museum; 89 above right, CHS Costume Collection; 89 below, USX Corporation; 90 above, Myrtle West; 90 below, Helene Curtis Industries, Inc.; 91, Copyright 1942, Chicago Tribune Company, all rights reserved, used with permission; 92, Mid-West Company; 93 above, The Hon. Mary G. Sethness; 93 below, Library of Congress; 94, The Franklin D. Roosevelt Library; 95, CHS Prints and Photographs Collection.

The Crossroads City

96, postcard, "I Just Joined Up," Paul R. Nordskog; 96, postcard packet, "U.S. Naval Training Station," Marie Maracek; 96, broadside, "Get Him Off Lonesome Street," CHS Library; 96, photograph, Union Station concourse, Library of Congress; 96, defense bond stamp album, "My Victory Book," Peggy Tagliere; 97, James Norton; 98 above and below, CHS Prints and Photographs Collection; 99, Todd Stump; 100 right, Library of Congress; 101, poster, "Volunteer For Victory," CHS Prints and Photographs Collection; 101, blood donor certificate, Marilou Cosgrove; 101, program, "Hollywood Victory Caravan," Jeanette P. Latman; 101, poster, "High School Grad's/Fly With The Navy," Richard Bitterman; 102, program, "Weapons of War," Peter Johnsen; 102, poster, "Hit The Beach!", Idair and Ronald Taradash; 102, photograph, Army War Show, Chicago Park District Special Collections; 102, ticket, "Pacific Theater," Bob Van Pelt; 103 left, Chicago & Northwestern Historical Society; 104 above, Library of Congress; 104 middle and below, The University of Chicago Library, Department of Special Collections; 105 above and below, CHS Prints and Photographs Collections; 106, Northwestern University Library Archives; 107 above, Chicago Park District Special Collections; 107 below, CHS Prints and Photographs Collection; 108 above, Perry R. Duis; 108 below, Chicago Jewish Archives; 109, Idair and Ronald Taradash; 110, Chicago Park District Special Collections; 111 above left and right, CHS Prints and Photographs Collections; 111 below, Chicago Park District Special Collections; 112 above, CHS Prints and Photographs Collection; 112 below, National Archives; 113 left, Mary Alice Smith; 113 right, Chicago Park District Special Collections.

Inventing the Postwar World

114, photographs, CHS Prints and Photographs Collection; 114, postcard, "I've learned a lot of knots," Paul R. Nordskog; 114, cartoon, Copyright, *Chicago Tribune* Company, all rights reserved, used with permission; 115, CHS Prints and Photographs Collection; 117, Chicago Public Library; 118 below, from *Men and Events*, CHS Library; 119 left, from *South Shore Country Club Magazine*, July 1945, CHS Library; middle, photograph by Mildred Mead, CHS, ICHi-18300; 119 below, The University of Chicago Library, Department of Special Collections; 120, Chicago Public Library.

Index

Illustrations are indicated in italics. If a subject is illustrated and discussed on the same page, the illustration is not separately indicated